When I Die

When I Die

Lessons from the Death Zone

PHILIP GOULD

Edited by Keith Blackmore

Little, Brown

LITTLE, BROWN

First published in Great Britain in 2012 by Little, Brown
Reprinted 2012 (twice)

A CIP catalogue record for this book
is available from the British Library.

ISBN 978-1-4087-0398-4

Typeset in Bembo by M Rules
Printed and bound in Great Britain by
Clays Ltd, St Ives plc

Papers used by Little, Brown are from well-managed forests
and other responsible sources.

MIX
Paper from
responsible sources
FSC® C104740

Little, Brown
An imprint of
Little, Brown Book Group
100 Victoria Embankment
London EC4Y 0DY

An Hachette UK Company
www.hachette.co.uk

www.littlebrown.co.uk

To all the staff at the Royal Marsden Hospital, London
and the Royal Victoria Infirmary, Newcastle

Contents

Foreword   1

The Glory of the Ride   9
The Courage of the Small   29
A Very Small Boat   45
The Bottom of a Murky Sea   67
The Unfinished Life   81
The Cancer Odyssey   93
The Tall Black Cloud   101
The Death Zone   117
Going to my Grave   137

Four Days Left to Change the World:
    Georgia Gould   145

My Dad: *Grace Gould*   179
Postscript: *Gail Rebuck*   182
Letter to a Friend: *Alastair Campbell*   205

Acknowledgements   209

A Short Introduction to Oesophageal/
     Gastro-oesophageal Cancers   215
Obituary: *The Times*   219
Cast   227

Foreword

I first met Philip Gould on 15 June 2011. James Harding, the editor of *The Times*, and I arrived at his house near Regent's Park expecting to find a man on the edge of death. In fact we found someone full of life, who had that very day been given hope that he might have as long as another eighteen months to live. He was cheerful and gregarious and looking forward to a holiday in Italy with his wife, Gail Rebuck.

We had come because he had written the long and detailed account of his treatment for cancer of the oesophagus that makes up the early chapters of this book. He was keen that it should receive as wide an audience as possible. At more than twenty thousand words it was a difficult proposition – too long for conventional serialisation, too short for a book – but he wanted *The Times* to publish it. What he had written was so powerful that James decided to print every word, four pages a day for a week.

We settled on trying to give each instalment a cliff-hanging end, so people would want to return the next day to find out what happened next. Philip enjoyed this idea of treating his work almost as if it were a thriller. We decided to call the series *The Unfinished Life*, thereby giving a nod to Philip's magisterial political book, *The Unfinished Revolution*.

Philip took a very active part in the serialisation, bombarding us with emails, insisting on writing all the picture captions and reading all the proofs. He and Gail also gave a moving interview to Janice Turner for *The Times Magazine*.

The serial was extremely well received and readers of *The Times* left Philip in no doubt of their appreciation. The message boards and our letters department were inundated.

Philip departed on his holiday a couple of weeks later, planning to add another twenty pages to a new edition of *The Unfinished Revolution*. In fact he provided another 140 as he brought the book up to date.

We agreed to serialise that too and every now and then he and I would exchange emails about his progress. In September the proofs arrived, but by then it was clear that Philip's cancer had returned.

This in no way diluted his enthusiasm for the new project. Once again he wanted to be involved at every level, arguing with me about the headlines and nagging us relentlessly to make sure his message was put across accurately. He also talked about his plans to continue the work he had begun with *The Unfinished Life*, to write an account not only of his cancer but also the next phase of his treatment and the growing certainty of his own death.

He describes in these pages how at first he could find no purpose in knowing that he was about to die, a terrible moment for someone whose life had been built on the idea of having goals and creating the strategies to achieve them. But then he found that purpose: writing and talking about confronting death in ways that would not only comfort his family but help strangers too.

When he and his great friend Alastair Campbell were planning political campaigns they had a saying: 'Strategy is not strategy unless it is written down.' Philip's new strategy was to deal with his own imminent death. And so he wanted to write it down. Naturally the newspaper wanted to know more about this too, so he and I began to exchange emails again, this time with me doing the nagging.

But his illness and its treatment were not so obliging now. Philip entered the Death Zone, as he put it, and although he was still writing, the words did not come as quickly as they had done before.

He also gave some remarkable interviews. In one with Andrew Marr for the BBC on 18 September he spoke frankly about his cancer and its likely outcome. He talked about being in the Death Zone and his calmly courageous acceptance of his imminent death caused a considerable stir.

Two days later another interview appeared, this one by Simon Hattenstone in the *Guardian*. Again Philip spoke honestly about his illness, and he made the point forcibly that he had accepted death and was ready for it.

Philip's frankness in these interviews was disconcerting for his family – both had been given to publicise the republication of *The Unfinished Revolution*, not his illness – but it was also becoming clear that he was very determined to be outspoken about dying.

Amid all the treatment, and the debilitating effects of the illness itself, Philip continued to write, and if his words lacked the polish of his earlier efforts they were certainly not short of passion.

Towards the end of October he gave two long interviews to Adrian Steirn, an Australian photographer and film-maker who had been commissioned to make a short film about Philip. Adrian and his team also arranged to go with Philip to Highgate Cemetery to take the picture of Philip at his own graveside which can be found on the dust jacket of this book.

The two interviews Adrian filmed provided the material that makes up the bulk of the chapter called 'The Death Zone'. I have adapted them using Philip's notes and writings. He had barely a week to live as he spoke, but his energy seemed limitless and his thinking clear.

Philip continued writing until he could no longer use his laptop. He then started dictating his thoughts to Gail as she sat by his bedside in hospital. He outlined his ideas on the structure the book should have and listed chapter headings. Some of this material is understandably fragmented, but I have preserved as much of it as possible.

Once Philip entered intensive care five days before his death, only three people had continuous access to him, although he saw visitors and emailed and texted friends. Georgia Gould, Philip's elder daughter, undertook the difficult job of describing those last days in her chapter of this book. Grace Gould has provided a snapshot of her relationship with her father and Gail Rebuck surveys in a postscript the four-year history of Philip's illness and this book's origins. The last word is left to Alastair Campbell, whose email to his closest friend in politics was read to Philip a few hours before he died and again at the funeral service.

Although his life was suffused with the world of British politics, particularly the Labour Party, no political affiliations are required to appreciate Philip Gould the man. He had in abundance one of life's most underrated qualities: enthusiasm. His sense that things *can* be done informed everything he did, from politics to family and friends, even to Queens Park Rangers. Warm and open even towards complete strangers, he was staunch and loyal to his friends and decent and fair-minded to his opponents. It was noticeable after his death that some of the

most moving tributes came from the other side of the
political fence.

As he had wrestled with the terrors and trials of his illness, however, he had begun to see a public duty in this
private struggle too. He wanted to inform and comfort, to
combat what he saw as the ignorance and misapprehen-
sion, not to mention the fear, he had found surrounding
the issue of cancer and its treatment.

An experience of death when Philip was younger had
already left a powerful and lasting impression on him – he
had been with his father when he died. 'The last words I
heard him say were, "That is my son and I am proud of
him." I was determined to justify that pride.' Philip had
been distressed by his father's last hours, noticing how he
had struggled to breathe, and his fear of the rattle he heard
then was to come back to haunt him as his own illness
reached its final stages.

Once Philip himself had entered the Death Zone he
decided to explore and map this new territory. He walked
around its perimeter and he marched right into its mys-
terious centre. This book is his last great campaign. The
fact that it is written by one of the most influential political figures of the past twenty years is irrelevant. It is true
that prime ministers and other giants of recent public life
do occasionally flit across its pages, but they always do so
as friends rather than politicians.

This is not a book about politics. It is a book about

cancer and dying. It is the story of a man and his illness, his family and friends, his doctors and nurses. At its heart are his wife Gail and daughters Georgia and Grace, whom he loved above all else.

Keith Blackmore

The Glory of the Ride

It starts at ten o'clock on Tuesday 29 January 2008 in a private clinic in London . . .

I am lying on my side at the mid-point of an endoscopy, sedated but fully conscious, hearing the quiet hum of medical conversation as the endoscope gradually eases down my gullet, displaying all it sees on television screens. I prefer not to watch.

Until now all has gone well, the voices calm and subdued, but then it is as though a goal has been scored at Wembley, the room exploding with noise and energy: they have discovered a cancer, and I hear the word 'big'. They talk as if I am not there, a bystander at my own demise.

Eventually the endoscope is removed and the doctor

tells me with barely concealed excitement that they have found a growth that is certain to be a malignant tumour and that it is large. I fear the uncertainty more than the diagnosis. 'What are my chances?' I ask. 'Fifty-fifty,' he replies and I feel a combination of shock and hope. Not great, but better odds than I thought they might be. I have a chance.

Suddenly a surgeon arrives as if from nowhere. He quickly inspects the images and tells me that it is a junction cancer situated between my oesophagus and my stomach. In a second I have lost control of my world.

I am wheeled out of the operating theatre and return to my cubicle, now a cancer patient. My wife, Gail Rebuck, rushes in, her face full of love and hope, certain that I will be all right. Just an hour ago I had been told that the chances of cancer were remote and I had phoned to reassure her. It was a mistake to have done so, creating false hope.

I tell her the new truth, harshly because I am nervous, and she almost physically recoils, as though punched in the stomach. She says that it will all be fine but does not believe it. I phone my daughter Georgia who is doing some research in Manchester and she is stunned, unable to take in the information. Gail takes the phone and leaves the room to talk to her. I can hear them through the door; it is clear that they are both in floods of tears. I am not the victim here.

We drive home in silence. Gail is distant; she sees the

contours of her life shifting in front of her. I feel guilty. I
have let her down.

I made an immediate decision to be as open and honest as
I possibly could about what had happened, reaching out to
people rather than trying to do it alone. I needed help but
I also had to give help. I do not consider myself someone
who naturally leads, and if I do so at all it is by creating a
shared spirit, pushing forward with enthusiasm and energy.
But this was different, I now had an explicit responsibility to lead. I was reliant on the support of others, but they
too were relying on me.

I started calling and the conversations went well. I
sensed affection and it immediately lifted me. I thought, if
only I had known they liked me so much before I got ill.
Mostly they said one of two things: 'You are too happy to
have got cancer,' or 'You are so strong you are bound to
get through.' The first assumption had already been proved
wrong; I hoped the second would not be.

The first call after getting home was to my younger
daughter Grace, who was in Oxford. I did not want to tell
her the news over the phone, so I said that we would be
coming up that evening to see her. I told her that it was
serious, but I wanted to speak to her face to face. This was
not perfect but it was the best that I could do.

My sister, Jill, was shaken but full of kindness; she is a
priest and she found the right words. Gail's parents were
beside themselves, difficult to console. Peter Jones, my

closest friend from our days at the University of Sussex, was as always incurably optimistic, but I could feel his anxiety.

Alastair Campbell was stunned. His life had already been touched by cancer, and now he was seeing another of his closest friends and political colleagues fall prey to the disease. But he was, as always in a crisis, totally solid and absolutely loyal. Nothing is too much for him at a moment like this.

Afterwards he called Georgia to reassure her. She later told me that when I called she had felt complete panic, never having considered the possibility of my death or even illness. She was devastated, almost hysterical, walking aimlessly around the streets of Manchester until Alastair called her. Our children had grown up together and were as close as family, and Calum, Alastair's younger son, who was in Manchester at university, found her and stayed with her. Together they brought her back to life.

Matthew Freud, whose company I had just joined, reassured me that whatever happened he would stand by me, a constant friend. Anji Hunter gave me an uncompromising blast of Middle England fortitude, just as she had done so many times before as Tony Blair's 'gatekeeper'. Peter Hyman, a Blair strategist who left Downing Street to become a teacher, reacted with all his normal compassion and integrity. In the 1997 election we had jointly created the Labour Pledges, and had become very close.

Then I called Downing Street, something I had once done often but which rarely happened now. But 'Switch', as the switchboard is known, remembered me and the telephonist was kind, sensing something was wrong. The next day I was due to make a presentation to Gordon Brown on public perceptions of him based on some polling that I had done. I got through to someone deep in his office and said that I would be unable to do it because I had been diagnosed with cancer. Within minutes Gordon phoned back, his deep gravelly voice betraying genuine concern. This was the first of many calls he would make. The presentation went ahead without me: the findings about him were harsh and I felt guilty for inflicting them on him.

That was how the day went, calling and being called. I knew that one part of me enjoyed being the centre of attention, and while wary of this, I was prepared to use it to help get me through.

At about six we drove to Oxford. Resilient as ever, Gail had recovered. It was a quiet, reflective journey; mostly we were worrying about how Grace would take the news. When we arrived she was standing confidently outside her college, looking cool and contained. I said straight away that I had serious cancer and her response was typical – blunt with an edge of humour: 'I knew when you phoned that either you had cancer or you and Mum were getting a divorce.'

We had dinner, which was warm and close, but with an

undercurrent of anxiety, and I was very sad to leave her. Gail and I drove back without speaking much.

So the first day with cancer ended.

That night I woke and for a moment felt fear and panic, black thoughts attacking like demons. A survival instinct kicked in and I treated my fears almost like a video game, repelling each negative impulse one by one, turning them from dark to light. This worked well enough, and the demons never got through. (In time I was to develop a crude form of meditation and used simple affirmations that worked almost all the time. I learnt how to change my mood, a basic skill of cancer survival.)

The next day I returned to the London Clinic to meet Satvinder Mudan, the surgeon who had suddenly appeared during my fateful endoscopy. He was young, energetic and articulate, and enjoyed the ebb and flow of argument. Like many surgeons he took the glass-half-empty approach to life: the operation would involve a great deal of pain, the worst of it three or four days in intensive care that would be noisy and unpleasant, survival and cure a long way from guaranteed.

After a couple of sessions he gave my wife a copy of a book he had edited on cancer of the oesophagus; it was full of colour pictures of rather horrible-looking tumours of various kinds; worse, it claimed the survival rate was less than 10 per cent. Perfect bedtime reading for Gail.

This was the first I had heard of oesophageal cancer,

which I now know to be the solid cancer with the most rapidly increasing number of cases in the world at present, and one of the most lethal.

It is impossible to know when my cancer started. From a young age my stress had revealed itself through my stomach, and gastric pains had been a feature of my life. A doctor told me that my form of oesophageal cancer often caused painful symptoms when first established, but then lay low, perhaps for years, with few if any symptoms until it was too late. That is why the cancer is so lethal.

This description fitted my pattern exactly: I had experienced a short phase of acute discomfort, but this had passed and been replaced by low-level indigestion, and a slight cough when I ate. Enough to worry me now and again, but never enough to persuade me to confront the issue and have an endoscopy. I knew I should have done it, but I never quite did.

Satvinder made clear my position: if the cancer had spread I would not survive, but if it had not, then cure was possible. The next week would involve numerous tests to see if we could advance to surgery. I liked him. He was confident and sharp, and from where I was sitting he was all I had. I wanted help now. And he was fast and very competent.

That same day I was to have a CT scan, then in the following days a laparoscopy, a PET scan and an endoscopic ultrasound. Tests I had never previously heard of were to govern my future.

Back home the flow of calls had become a flood, and the house was filling with flowers. I wrote in my diary at the time that 'I felt engulfed by a tidal wave of love from dozens and dozens of people, and this love has an almost physical power, lifting me up during all the bad moments and carrying me through. At night I can almost feel the power of prayer.' Peter Mandelson called with a typically stringent view: 'It will be tough but other people have got through it and so will you.' He was right, of course, as he often is.

On Thursday, Tony Blair visited, and so began an entirely new phase in our relationship. Until then we had been friends and colleagues, close but in a way constrained. Cancer was to change that. At that first meeting he displayed an emotion I had not seen before, saying that he had taken me for granted, had acknowledged my contribution but not fully appreciated it. I felt this was not just about me but about him, this brush with cancer releasing emotions that office and the negativity of public life had in some ways silenced.

And there was another reason too. Tony is a deeply religious person, imbued with a strong sense of values, but he believes that these values, and his religious conviction, belong properly to a private realm, not the public world that dominated so much of his life. He made a kind of distinction between Church and State, and is in that way a secular politician.

But with my cancer we had left the public world and

were living completely in the private realm, and his compassion, his religion and his values could in a way be
liberated. What is certain is that he could not have been
more assiduous in his support for me and my family
throughout my illness, contacting me almost daily for
much of its duration.

This division between public and private life is the fate
of all politicians. They are constantly scrutinised but only
rarely understood. I mention political people often in
these pages, partly because they are my friends and are
intrinsic to the story, but also because I want to show what
they are like out of the limelight, acting as private individuals, and how, without exception, they never let me
down.

The next Monday I returned to the hospital and was given
the results of the tests. Satvinder said I had a carcinoma of
the gastro-oesophageal junction, that the type of my cancer
was adenocarcinoma (the type associated with high-stress,
middle-aged, middle-class living, i.e. you lot reading this
now!), and that it was about five centimetres wide at its
maximum. There was no evidence that it had spread and
we could now proceed to chemotherapy.

On Satvinder's advice I decided to be treated by
Maurice Slevin at the London Oncology Centre. By now
I was fully immersed in the private system, something that
caused my daughter Georgia great distress. She said I
should stick to the National Health Service. In my heart

I knew she was right, but for the moment I was clinging to the certainty of what I knew. I was using private medicine partly for rational, partly for emotional reasons. I had got into the habit of having my regular health tests carried out privately after my GP had told me that he did not believe in preventative testing, considering it to be counter-productive.

When I first noticed a difficulty in swallowing and knew I had a potential problem, I went instinctively and immediately to a private clinic which diagnosed the cancer and charted the way forward. Of course I could have changed direction but at that moment I was nervous of disruption, and at some deeper level anxious about the NHS. This was to change, but not for a while. I wanted security.

Maurice Slevin was an energetic South African who my wife rather disconcertingly described as dashing. Everything about him was high-tech and modern, with no trace of the genteel comfort that is normally the hallmark of private medicine. He was confident, articulate and impressive, and helped me through this early period. He made it clear that almost certainly the chemotherapy would not be as difficult and frightening as I thought it might be.

He explained that I would undergo the standard protocol for oesophageal cancer, called the MAGIC trial, which had been developed in the UK and was now used around the world. This meant three sessions before and three after the surgery with a combination of drugs called

EOX (epirubicin, oxaliplatin and capecitabine). I would probably lose my hair, but even that was not certain if I used something called a cold cap that would freeze my head during treatment (which, it was to turn out, was the worst thing about the whole process).

The actual chemotherapy was done in a light and friendly basement, with each patient sitting in one of what looked like a pair of airline seats. My first treatment was on 12 February. It started at about nine in the morning and consisted of a series of intravenous drips that were fed into my body through a 'port', which had already been inserted via a minor operation.

First came a water flush, then anti-sickness drugs, then the two chemo drugs; a third was to be taken in tablet form at home. None of this hurt or was unpleasant, although I was disturbed to find that the second drug turned my pee a horrible bright red. The treatment was strong and I could immediately feel the power of the drugs moving through my body. Still, I felt I would be able to cope with it.

Gail came and sat with me for hours during these ses-sions, as did Sally Morgan. Sally used to run the Blair political office, where her friendliness and huge warmth belied a hidden toughness. She had protected Tony in the tough middle period of his prime ministership, and was a constant support to me.

Meanwhile, I was focusing on the serious matter of fighting the cancer. Georgia had bought me the complete speeches of Churchill and I listened to them as I ran on a running machine, trying to get fit for the operation.

Everything I thought about the battle with cancer was strategic, as if I were fighting an election campaign. I saw the elimination of the cancer as victory, and the test results as opinion polls. Alastair Campbell called the cancer Adolf, and me Churchill.

People might have thought I was mad, and in a way I probably was, but that was how I felt, how I had always lived my life. I loved politics, and loved elections even more. My first had been in 1987 and I expected my last to be in 2010, although I always hoped privately to do more. But above all I loved to think, to strategise, to solve the unanswerable political problem. And this is what I was doing now, thinking constantly, not just about how to get through, but about the best way of getting through.

For me strategy is not a static thing, but fluid and ever changing. As my time passed I was to become, I hope, stiller, and calmer and more reflective, reacting in new ways to the new demands of cancer. But my instinct is always the same: identify the problem and find the way forward. In the end, of course, there may not be one, but that moment, too, will have its own answer.

As the surgery got closer I had to put my affairs in order. I made a will and organised my funeral. This sounds far worse than it is. The very process of working out the order of service and the music dispels anxiety. When Gail and I went to see the vicar to discuss all this, we rowed horribly all the way there. But, when faced with the reality of the funeral, we immediately grew calm. We felt this was a small defeat for death.

Although my treatment at the London Clinic and the London Oncology Centre had been exemplary I became convinced it was time to move on; I wanted to get back to the NHS. My first instinct was to go to the Royal Marsden Hospital, but they had just suffered a major fire and I was told by someone attached to the hospital that surgery there would not be advisable for a while. I spoke to many senior consultants within the NHS – Ara Darzi, the distinguished cancer surgeon, was particularly helpful at this time, on an entirely informal basis – and was given names and hospitals, but could find no consensus as to where I should go.

One day I asked a leading NHS consultant where I should go for my best possible life chance. He answered without pausing for thought: Murray Brennan at the Memorial Sloan-Kettering Cancer Center in New York City. And he was not alone in saying so. In the end, after endless discussion and investigation, we arrived at two options, both of which we believed to be equally valid: a well-respected surgeon at a London teaching hospital and Memorial Sloan-Kettering. The advice I had been given was generous, impeccably fair and informed throughout. But in the end the decision was mine, and I take full responsibility for it.

I went to see both surgeons. The NHS consultant was

charming and proposed a radical course of action. He wanted to perform what is called an oesophago-gastrectomy, in which the tumour would be fully removed. He sought to do this not just by entry through the stomach but by cracking open my ribs and gaining access through the chest. He believed in taking out as much of the stomach and as many lymph nodes as possible. He told me there would be pain and discomfort and it would be tough, but that patients get through it and it is worth it for the improved life chance. I liked him, but felt uneasy. I was not sure, and planned to visit New York.

On 21 April Gail and I walked to Memorial Sloan-Kettering in New York City in the spring sunshine. The hospital soared above us like a vast office block, right in the middle of Manhattan, with a reception that was more corporate than medical. Above us was floor after floor offering what appeared to be an infinite variety of cancer specialisms, like a great cancer department store.

I arrived at Murray Brennan's floor expecting the atmosphere to be like a typical British private hospital: faded, plush and very quiet. It was the opposite, utilitarian rather than comfortable, reflecting both the harshness of New York and the ethos of the hospital, which is to kill cancer whatever it takes. And far from being quiet it was heaving with people, waiting largely to see Murray himself. They were less like patients waiting to see a doctor, more like pilgrims coming to see a healer.

In any event we waited a long time, far longer than in any other hospital before or since, and we finally met Murray only for a short time. But in that period he was impressive, even if he also seemed to be holding back. He is a New Zealander not an American, taciturn to the point of coolness – at least at first meeting. He has had a hugely distinguished career, having been chairman of the surgery practice at Memorial Sloan-Kettering for more than twenty years.

He told us my cancer was very serious but that he was confident there was a good chance of fixing it. He was proud of his hospital and its high survival rates, putting this down not to any single factor but to a connected system of excellence. And he said that Memorial Sloan-Kettering was not a private hospital but an endowment hospital, seeing 20 per cent of its patients on a not-for-profit basis.

In contrast to what we had heard in the UK he preached moderation rather than radicalism. I would not go to intensive care but straight to a recovery room. He would perform a full resection (removal of the tumour), but he intended to confine entry to the stomach and avoid secondary access through the chest, which he was strongly against.

Gail liked his approach because she considered it a more moderate, sensible option and she disliked my predilection for extremism. But she was not relaxed about going to the United States and was nervous about the possibility that the care would be fragmented and dislocated. I liked it because it seemed the boldest option, offering the best chance of survival and the lowest level of discomfort.

The hospital was impressive but the atmosphere felt unyielding and hard; it was disconcerting to see Gail paying by credit card there and then. It was efficient rather than warm.

Once we were back in the UK we were unsure and ungrounded, not knowing what to do. Our problem was not just that we were uncertain, but that we were making our decision in a kind of no man's land, connected to the NHS but not really part of it. Although I had regained contact with NHS consultants I had not connected properly with the NHS system. I had left one harbour, but failed properly to reach another.

So I gave it my best shot and asked everyone I respected, including all the right NHS people, what I should do. The view was pretty unanimous: Memorial Sloan-Kettering was an excellent facility and probably the best choice. There was no agreement at all on a preferred NHS equivalent.

And in the end, if New York offered the best chance of life, I felt almost morally obliged to go there. I felt at ease in America, having visited it many times, and having grown fond of it while working on Bill Clinton's 1992 election campaign. I decided to be bold. We were going to New York. Gail was not so sure. She thought I was being stubborn. But she respected my decision.

The surgery was scheduled for 1 May, exactly eleven

years after the general election victory of 1997. I considered this to be a good omen, but I was growing increasingly anxious. The date cast a shadow over the future, and every day it moved closer. My fear was less what would happen, more its inevitability. There would be no escape.

Spring gave way to early summer and it was time to leave for New York. Gail had to come out later so I flew there alone, then took a yellow cab through the city, something I had done many times before. I felt secure in the familiarity of the New York landscape and drew comfort from the fact that I still had a week to go, but deep down my anxiety was slowly growing.

This was New York, but it was not quite the New York I had always known. I was a patient, not a tourist. It was as if my vision had become blurred.

I checked into an apartment hotel on 64th Street. The staff were not welcoming but I had a small balcony overlooking the city and although I was alone, I was not lonely. I welcomed the privacy. Each day I got up and spent an hour or so in the gym, did my breathing exercises and walked in Central Park.

The kids had packed photos of the family which I put up, and given me a Zen Dog T-shirt to wear on the day of the surgery. It read:

He knows not where he's going for the ocean will decide,
It's not the destination it's the glory of the ride.

Those words pretty much summed up my position.

In the coming days I had a CT scan and an endoscopy, which were both done to a high level of expertise and care.

I went to see Murray Brennan again. He was more approachable this time, if still a little brusque. He said he wanted to treat the surgery as a stomach cancer rather than an oesophageal cancer, and repeated that above all he wanted to avoid breaking into the chest. He only wanted to make entry through the stomach.

I talked to a nurse about what it was going to be like on the day. She said that I would just walk into the hospital on the morning of the operation, spend a couple of hours in a holding room with my wife and then walk alone down a long corridor to the vast operating theatre. It sounded like the last walk of a condemned man. She helpfully suggested I might like to take a tranquilliser before I started.

Gordon Brown phoned me in New York, asking how long the operation was likely to be. I said, 'Six to eight hours,' and he replied: 'That will not be bad, that was the length of the operation on my eyes.' I had never heard Gordon speak like that before or since. It was a moment of complete connection.

The day before the surgery I wrote letters to each member of my family in the unlikely but nonetheless possible event that I did not make it through. I completely broke down doing this. It was agony.

Gail arrived that afternoon. She was, and is, CEO of the publishers Random House, and was under huge strain at work. It was incredible that she was now to stay with me in New York for two months, working in her company's New York office. I did not think I deserved that.

She busied herself making the flat into a kind of makeshift home and we talked continually. It was a night of unimaginable closeness. Cancer is the cause of so much distress but it is also the source of great intimacy. Never will I forget that time.

On the day of the operation I woke hollow with anxiety, but also with an edge of excitement. I put on my T-shirt and we left ridiculously early, walking to the hospital, inevitably getting lost and gently rowing about it. We took the elevator and made our way to the holding room. Murray arrived wearing a bright red bandana. He gripped me in a bear hug. 'Now it's up to me to save you,' he said, and in that moment I felt his power and his warmth.

Another hour and a half went past and it was time.

I walked with Gail for twenty yards or so and then she fell away and I was on my own. I entered the operating theatre, which was vast and glittering, with video screens hanging from the ceiling, and in the middle a small bed, utterly dwarfed by the epic scale of the stage. Murray ignored me, scrubbing up in the corner. I climbed on to the bed, and the anaesthetist put me out of my misery.

The Courage of the Small

Above me I saw a bright and shining light and I knew I was alive.

I gulped in the elation. I was alive and just felt immense relief. Gail came in and I talked to her and called the kids. Grace was worried. Georgia was happy. I did not sleep at all that night, watching television on a high of adrenalin.

I cannot remember ever feeling quite so happy. But this happiness was an illusion produced in part by steroids. In the morning I moved to my permanent home within the hospital, a small, sparse, stark room which I was to share with a volatile New Yorker who rarely stopped talking. There was no window. It was, of course, fine but a room designed for utility not satisfaction.

Gail described to me what the day had been like for her:

hell. Waiting with no information until finally Murray Brennan appeared, his white coat stained with blood, looking exhausted, as though he had been battling a whale. He said the operation had been incredibly tough, and that he had battled to avoid breaking through my ribs. He had struggled to rejoin the two ends of the oesophagus from which the tumour had been cut out.

Murray wrote at the time: 'We performed an oesophago-gastrectomy on Lord Gould today. We were able to do it from the abdomen, but it was a high anastomosis so we need to follow him closely.' It was clearly a tough op, for him as well as me.

I settled into my new room and started to fade. I had tubes everywhere, including one in my nose. My face drained of colour and I went a dreadful shade of white. Gail said I looked more dead than alive. She hated it there, the room, the thin curtain that separated me from my room-mate, my appalling appearance, the strangeness of it all. For several days I could not drink, only suck on cotton-tipped sticks dipped in water.

Then there was the problem of language and communication. Because of the dryness of my mouth and the tube in my nose, I could barely talk and much of what I did manage to say was unintelligible. Most of the nurses could not understand what I was talking about and clearly suspected that I was being inhospitable. By contrast, all the New Yorker had to do was grunt and he seemed to be immediately understood.

The day was bad but the night was worse, the morphine turning the hours into a terrible, ever-moving nightmare of fears and dark forces. During this period my room never seemed to be still – it was always moving, shifting, contorting and somewhat threatening me. This was what the nights became: endless New York banter and a moving inchoate darkness.

The next day my spirits slipped further. I woke up feeling bereft of energy and the pain of the operation was starting to wear me down. I felt that the only way to cope was to retreat and conserve whatever energy I had.

In my head I called this – rather absurdly – the lizard strategy. Hunker down, hide, retreat. It did not work. It sent a signal to my surgeon and the nurses that I lacked the firepower to see the process through, and by sending out no energy it meant that less came back to me.

Murray became convinced that my low mood was the consequence of a leak – a failure of the surgery to join the various parts perfectly – and immediately ordered a CT scan. This involved my drinking a contrast liquid, which was no fun at all, and holding a position during the scan that was, so soon after the surgery, even worse. There was no leak but I learnt my lesson. I work best when I am positive, and when I am not things get worse rather than better. From that moment on my recovery accelerated and confidence in me improved. I was on the way up.

From day two, even after major surgery like this, the

medical staff insisted on mobility, effectively to stop fluid accumulating in my lungs. This, it was hoped, would lessen the risk of pneumonia.

Mobility means walking, and somehow or other they got me out of my bed, attached all my tubes and bottles and drains to a frame and sent me off on what I called the walk of death: a seemingly endless journey around the inner core of the building. Each step was a huge effort, a full walk round the block an eternity. At first I had to do it five times. Then ten. Then twenty.

I was not alone in this enterprise. Other patients who had had the same or similar operations were also walking, all looking more like apparitions than people, washed out, white-faced, haunted. No one spoke, no one even smiled. We just walked on, like ghosts.

But for all the misery of the walk of death, day by day things got better. One by one, the drains and tubes were removed, and within a week I was walking normally and unaided, an incredible testament to the human body's powers of recovery.

Gail visited me twice a day for long periods, even though she was working flat out. She did not like the hospital, finding it harsh and unyielding. In a way she was right, but this brutality was also the hospital's strength. It was a cancer terminator, unwavering in its determination to cure the disease. It was New York and it was a tough place.

Each time Gail tried to get me moved from my shared room to one of the few single rooms on the floor she failed, always pre-empted by someone else. Then a nurse gave me the secret of success: the only way I could secure a room, she said, was to take all my possessions and just squat in one, which I did.

That is what it is like in a New York City hospital. But the longer I was there the more I liked it.

For a start I could talk rather than mumble through tubes and dryness. I got to know the nurses well, and they were exemplary – the nurses on my floor had been voted the best nursing staff in the north-east of the United States. The average time most of them had spent on this ward was more than ten years, and they were caring and efficient. They did not wear uniforms but jeans and T-shirts, and they were confident in their role.

The doctors, too, were excellent, many of them coming from all over the world as fellows for short periods to experience life at a major cancer hospital. They were sharp, bright and intellectually curious. I spent hours talking to them. I could not say I liked Memorial Sloan-Kettering, but I admired it.

About five days after my surgery, Murray bounded into my room with an enthusiasm that belied his previous coolness. 'We have your histology results and they are excellent,' he said. There were no cancer cells in any of the lymph nodes – I could start planning a second career.

He would not stop talking, saying his previous taciturnity reflected his fear that at least one of the nodes was contaminated with cancer, which would have significantly

affected my life chances. Now he was all optimism: I had
a 75 per cent chance of five-year survival.

I felt hope, and a softly growing excitement, the same
sense I have felt on so many occasions – and in so many
elections – that despite everything I had won through.

Two days later, as so often with cancer, a step forward was
followed by a step back. The surgery wound was looking
red and sore and Murray said it was infected. His response
to this was not to use antibiotics, which he disapproved of
because they encouraged MRSA, but to open the wound
and let it heal naturally. He was confident that it would be
healed in two or three weeks.

The infection introduced me to a process known as
packing, not my favourite moment on the cancer journey.
Packing involved pushing gauze into the open wound with
a kind of wooden spatula. The gauze was then pushed
down to the very bottom of the wound, and more gauze
was packed in until the wound was completely filled.
Although not painful, this was uncomfortable.

Almost worse was the pre-packing cleansing in which
I had to wash the open wound in a shower, not just exter-
nally but internally. I will not forget looking down at this
vast, gaping, blood-red wound that seemed to go so deep
into my body that I could not see its end, and then trying
to flood it with water.

This process was to be repeated twice a day, for more
than two months.

The day before I left hospital I needed to get my wound checked by one of the younger doctors. The only place they could do this was the outpatients department, effectively the hospital's A&E. This seemed to be the main point of contact with the hospital for those with fewer resources, possibly getting their treatment for free. It was a demanding place to be, functional at best, with little hint of comfort of any sort. Many of those in the waiting area were African American and many were showing signs of distress. One couple in particular stood out. He was in late middle age and had a feeding tube directly into his throat. He was in some pain and gasping for breath, making a harsh rasping sound that echoed round the room. His wife held him partly through love, partly through panic. I smiled at her but she looked at me blankly, no sign of a response.

After a while the doctor called him in and she was left alone, and she immediately responded with a huge smile. She said that these few moments alone gave her some relief, that when she was with him she simply could not relax. And she was with him, she said, almost all the time, day after day, night after night.

I began to understand what cancer meant for those without resources, without help, without insurance, without any kind of reliable medical support. These two were lucky, they were being treated, and in an outstanding institution. But what about those who were beyond the reach of such care, not just in the United States but elsewhere? Cancer is tough at any time; in poverty, without proper treatment and support, it must be hell on earth.

The next day I left the hospital, and walked into the warm mid-May sunshine. There was blossom on the trees, and it was impossible not to feel a moment of happiness – I had got through it and I had won.

We returned to the hotel and I attempted to get back to normal. But normality was not so easy to find. I went out to dinner and ate some chicken, which got stuck in my throat. I struggled home, with acute pain and occasional vomiting. It took two hours to clear the chicken from my throat. This happened time and time again. And if it was difficult for me, it was far worse for Gail.

Meanwhile the wound packing, done by two nurses from the hospital, continued twice a day. Each day followed its own routine. A walk to the park, a few futile attempts at eating, the evening spent watching the politics shows, which all focused on the US primary elections.

Of course I loved the constant, obsessive attention to the elections night after night. I favoured Hillary Clinton for political and personal reasons; working on her husband's 1992 campaign had been formative for me on almost every level. But I was confident Obama would win, it was his moment.

There was the occasional break in routine. Ed Victor, my literary agent and a good friend, visited and we watched on television the Champions League final between Chelsea and Manchester United in Moscow. But mainly it was politics and packing.

So my time in New York passed.

I flew back to London on 30 May. I was determined to move lock, stock and barrel into the Marsden, arranging to see Professor David Cunningham, head of the gastro-intestinal unit.

Before my appointment I saw my private oncologist, Maurice Slevin. He disagreed completely with Murray Brennan's prognosis. He said that the margins were small, and that his analysis showed a less than 40 per cent chance of five-year survival, not the 75 per cent suggested by Murray. He recommended radiation, flatly contradicting the advice I had received in New York.

Next I saw the NHS surgeon I had decided not to use. He was emphatic. The wrong operation had been done, too few lymph nodes had been removed, and I should have had a full resection entered through the ribs. He also said, for good measure, that my wound would take another four to six weeks to heal, and that I had a massive hernia, the wall of my stomach having effectively collapsed as a result of the infection and the open wound. Fixing it would require another, quite major operation.

This confused and frightened me but my experience was not untypical. Medical opinion is rarely unanimous; there are often differences, sometimes small, sometimes big. I told Murray what the surgeon and the oncologist had said and a fierce transatlantic email battle ensued. Murray was angry, certain that he was right. It felt like the revenge of the British. I backed Murray.

I liked the Marsden the moment I went into it. It is warm, friendly and welcoming, and looks and feels efficient. I had found that I preferred hospitals solely dedicated to cancer because of the shared sense of experience and purpose. Every patient is in the same boat, and every member of staff understands that.

After a while the Marsden became like home for me. Culturally it is a very long way from Memorial Sloan-Kettering which is obsessive, functional, populated by large numbers of outstanding consultants and clinicians, confident in its own excellence, relentlessly storming the cancer barricades.

The Marsden is small, but still manages to be rambling. It has an implicit philosophy that beating cancer is important but so is the quality of life of those involved in the struggle. It may not have the relentless consistency of Memorial Sloan-Kettering but, with its numerous world-class consultants, it has a kind of understated brilliance that often equals anything Sloan-Kettering has to offer.

It can be frustrating – internal communication is far from perfect – but its merits massively outshine any defects it might have. The Marsden is, of course, an NHS hospital, and although it receives 30 per cent of its revenue through private patients (of which I was one), this does not fundamentally affect the character of the institution.

Patients in the United States probably feel more empowered than they do here, and they are probably treated with more efficiency, but the culture at the Marsden is warmer, less transactional and much more egalitarian.

Professor David Cunningham is a world-leading oncologist and was in fact primarily responsible for the development of the MAGIC trial which has saved and extended so many lives. When we went to see him in early June he was wary. I had arrived at the Marsden in mid-treatment, after rejecting it for a hospital in the United States and chemotherapy in Harley Street. I suspected that he did not know quite what to make of this, and that he was not hugely impressed by our choices.

Though professional and obviously highly competent, David was reserved rather than warm at this first meeting. Impressions were deceptive because I was later to learn that he is a genuinely warm figure with an impressive capacity to inspire, but he reveals his strengths slowly. He has the knowledge and the skill to meet the moment: the right advice or the right insight pops out of him at just the right moment.

David was gracious enough to concede that Sloan-Kettering was an excellent hospital and that if I had to be given chemotherapy by anyone in London, the best person to take care of it would be Maurice Slevin. This was generous of him, but I knew I had some work to do.

He slightly changed my chemotherapy protocol, moving the pill capecitabine from two weeks out of three to a continuous daily intake. I was worried that I was not to have radiation as Maurice suggested; he said that he would not recommend it.

I asked him what my life chances were. He would not commit himself. He just said they were good. I left, I am sure, more impressed with him than he was with me.

I started my post-surgical chemotherapy and felt confident. I had done it before and would do it easily again. Thus I made one of the common mistakes with cancer, which is to take things for granted.

Although a little slower than it had been with Maurice, the process was efficient, and the nurses excellent. We arrived at nine and left at about five. It was a long day but manageable.

But when I got home it all felt different.

The first time around my body had easily absorbed the chemotherapy, but this time I felt its presence more acutely, my body suffused with chemicals. My feet and fingers tingled painfully, making it completely impossible to touch anything from the fridge, and after a while I felt almost controlled by the chemicals flowing through me. It was as though the sensation of the cold cap that I hated so much was now being applied to the rest of my body.

The challenge of chemotherapy is that it engulfs you; it is in you, in a way that is totally different from the pain and discomfort of surgery. It is possible to construct a mental barrier between your consciousness and the effects of surgery, but with chemotherapy any such barrier disappears. You fuse with your treatment, your blood becoming a kind of poison that reaches every part of you.

For the next couple of days the steroids kept me going but as the weekend developed I felt an acidic taste start to grow at the back of my throat, which led inevitably to sickness and vomiting. It became hard to take the pills, and harder still to eat. And my body felt distressed, as though I was permanently seasick. Then, as week three arrived, these difficulties eased somewhat and I began to relax.

The second cycle, however, proved much worse. The acid did not just enter my throat, it consumed it. The vomiting worsened and followed almost every attempt to eat. Getting each pill down was an ordeal and I would sit in a chair by the window, forcing the pills down one after another in a process that took the best part of an hour.

I was not living life in terms of days or hours but minutes, getting by almost second by second. This is the reality of the cancer fight: not some massive heroic battle but a thousand small skirmishes, tiny victories, winning the war one pill, one drink, one minute at a time. The courage of the small.

I slouched into my sofa, just fighting to get through it all, staring ahead, not able to eat, to talk much, even really to move. Gail later said that this was the worst time for her, with me lying white-faced and immobile, staring blankly ahead, a ghost.

The Marsden, quite understandably, wanted to reduce my chemotherapy protocol to make it slightly easier to tolerate. Determined not to compromise with my cancer in any way, I would not do it. But I was on the edge.

Things just kept getting worse. For the only time in the whole cancer process my spirits really began to sag. I was becoming a basket case.

Margaret McDonagh, the indomitable former General Secretary of the Labour Party, called. 'The chemotherapy is beating me,' I said. Margaret, who had always been the steel at the heart of New Labour, was clearly offended by this display of weakness and almost yelled at me, 'You have got that the wrong way round, Philip. The chemotherapy is not beating you, you are beating the chemotherapy.'

I was so terrified of her that I had no option but to start fighting back.

David Blunkett called, commanding me to be strong, insisting that nothing should stop me. When David spoke it was with a power that was almost visceral. You could feel the years of adversity that he had overcome, the courage that he had shown. He certainly gave me strength.

By this time I had an array of anti-nausea drugs that could fill a small pharmacy, with new ones added almost on a daily basis. But they were not working.

One day, a Saturday, I felt in the early evening that I was

losing sensation in my right arm, then my left, and soon my neck, face and mouth. I was gradually becoming paralysed. I started to panic, sure I was having a heart attack or stroke.

Virtually unable to talk, I grunted to Gail the rudiments of my position, and we drove over to the A&E department at University College Hospital (UCH), which was as packed and crowded as on any Saturday evening. I stood in the middle of the room unable to speak or to feel anything much in my face, neck and arms, swaying from side to side like a demented scarecrow. My face, Gail said, looked as if it had calcified, like a rictus.

She was behind a couple of people who had, I am sure, perfectly legitimate illnesses, but now nothing would stop her: 'He's having a heart attack and he's got cancer,' she shouted, and in a trice I was in a cubicle having an ECG and numerous other tests.

It took them just moments to establish that my symptoms were those of a reaction to one of the anti-sickness drugs. They injected an antidote. Within minutes the paralysis ebbed away and I returned to normal. UCH has been good to me, excellent in every crisis that I've faced.

In all of this the wound packing was still going on, with no immediate chance of conclusion. But by then Donna Louise Spencer had arrived. A senior palliative nurse at St Thomas' Hospital, she was doing some part-time agency work and at that moment she became my saviour.

Getting through cancer needs leadership, and it can

come from anywhere: receptionists, friends, doctors. It was Donna who led me through the next two weeks. She told me I was taking too many anti-sickness drugs and they should be rationed.

She was confident that there would be a symptom control consultant at the Marsden. And she found one – Dr Julia Riley, who was brilliant and took control of my anti-nausea treatment, giving me a machine that would continuously pump the appropriate drugs into my arm.

Somehow or other, I scraped through.

A Very Small Boat

The very day after my chemo regimen finished, Gail and I set off by Eurostar from St Pancras railway station – we had been told it would be unwise for me to fly – on a trip that would take us eventually to Venice. We changed trains in Paris and then shared a small and rattly carriage with a couple of tiny bunks that took us through the night. We woke as the train pulled into Venice; the sun was shining, the treatment for my oesophageal cancer was over and I was starting a new life.

This is the best time, but it is also in some ways the worst. One of the things that makes an initial diagnosis bearable is, strangely, the speed with which cancer patients go on to treatment, creating immediately a sense of struggle, purpose and endpoint. The moment the treatment ends, that endpoint vanishes, the supporting structure disappears. You are pretty much on your own.

I remember exactly my conflicting feelings: joy that the chemotherapy and surgery were over but also fear of what the future might hold. I felt I was in a very small boat, floating in a very large sea.

Of course there is help available to prepare you for this – the Marsden has a small unit dedicated to it – but you still feel very alone.

At the core of my fear was the possibility that the disease would recur. With my cancer the risk of recurrence is not evenly distributed but is heavily concentrated in the first two years, peaking at about a year. If you can get to two years you should make five; if you can make five you are considered cured.

I have lost count of the number of times doctors have drawn this graphically for me, shown me a huge peak of risk in the coming year or so, tapering off with remarkable speed to safety after two years. So the goal is to reach the end of those two years without recurrence. It does not sound long. But it feels like an eternity.

Just before the treatment ended I saw David Cunningham and we discussed the way forward. Basically, he told me, I could walk out of the door and restart my life, but I would have to have regular CT scans to assess my progress and to see if the cancer had returned. The first scan would be in September, the next in December and then they would be done at regular six-monthly intervals.

The scans are not troubling in themselves. What is distressing is the delivery of the test results. It is like receiving an opinion poll on the future of your life.

There is no easy way to do it. Gail and I would inevitably arrive early and wait to see David, struggling to hide our anxiety. Absolutely the worst part is the moment of entry into the waiting room. You greet the people there, at the same time examining their faces and body language for hints of their likely prognosis. It all happens so fast, and with a faint sense of unreality, as though in a dream.

If the news is good you will usually be told instantly that all is well. Conversely if doctors have bad news for you, they invariably start with some earnest chatter about your condition, move on to some spurious evidence of something that has gone well, then announce a huge 'but' that swallows the room. Gail learnt to hate nothing so much as the word 'but'.

The first test in September went well, but that was expected. The second, in December, was also good and I started to relax. David said the next scan was important, and before the next meeting in June we hovered around the door to his office in a state of something approaching panic. But this test, too, was good.

This took us to December 2009 – effectively the two-year test, and self-evidently a crucial scan, the gateway to the real possibility of cure. This time I am afraid I cheated, hovering around David's office door again and hearing him say that Philip's tests 'all look good'.

I did not tell Gail, so fearful had I become of imparting good news that might not be confirmed. We went in and this time David was seriously optimistic, it was as though he had won the lottery. He did not say that I was cured – he did not even imply it – but it was clear he felt I was really on my way.

'You need not come in again for another year,' he said, which was clearly a huge vote of confidence. I insisted on the normal six months, because by then I was both cautious and superstitious. But as Gail and I walked into the cold midwinter evening we felt we had done it. We had reached the two-year mark clear of cancer and now statistics were on my side. It was going to be OK.

And so I got on with my life. Almost immediately I flew to the United States for meetings, probably far too quickly for my own good. I had a wonderful holiday in Jamaica at Christmas, healed by the sun, the heat and the breeze. I pitched into work, going to Freud's most days and quietly keeping going with my politics. I was determined to get back on track.

I did change my routine, if only partially. I took exercise every morning, and meditated every day. I moved from being inchoately spiritual to more emphatically religious. I was confirmed into the Church of England, after a couple of months of classes, and All Saints Margaret

Street became a place of sanctuary for me. I even took a course in philosophy at Birkbeck, University of London.

But I continued to work very hard, travelling to the United States on many occasions. My work was satisfying, and much of it fed off my experience of cancer, but by the end of the year I knew I was slipping out of balance.

Our twenty-fifth wedding anniversary would be in 2010 and so we spent Christmas in southern Kerala, India, where we had taken our honeymoon. I meditated twice a day with a local guru, and went often to local, unspoiled ashrams. I began to calm down. It was not to last. The general election was coming up and I was determined to contribute to it. I felt this was the time for people like me to stand up and be counted.

Gail was growing worried. She hated my involvement in politics, believing that it had been the root cause of my cancer. She began to see in me again the lack of energy and the torpor she associated with the original diagnosis. She wrote me a note begging me to slow down, saying, 'It is so heart-rending to see you destroy yourself like this. Nothing is worth that, nothing. At the centre of it all is politics, which is such a destructive force. It nearly killed you once, please don't let it kill you again.'

Gail had almost a sixth sense about me and my illness, always knowing when something was wrong. She had been right about everything connected to my cancer. And she was not alone. At around the same time, Grace texted me a very similar message: 'STOP. You are being an idiot.

You need to chill out and rest. You owe it to Mum who did so much for you when you were ill. It's not fair to let her stress now. You have a perfect excuse not to be involved in this politics stuff. You just don't have the stomach for it any more. (Yes I am that funny!)'

I was clearly doing something wrong.

For our actual twenty-fifth wedding anniversary we went to Jordan, and it was wonderful. But even while there I was dictating scripts for election broadcasts back to the campaign headquarters, something I kept quiet about when Gail was near.

When we returned home I tried to work on the campaign in a way that was effective while also being protective of my health. That was hard, because I love politics so much. I was determined not to let Labour down, but in truth I was getting tired, and my contribution was symbolic as much as practical.

Halfway through the election I flew to the United States to make a speech, and got trapped there by the cloud of volcanic dust which grounded planes across the world for a few days. To be stuck on the other side of the Atlantic was frustrating, even humiliating – but it forced me to rest and begin to reassess. I saw it as a sign that I had to change. But it was a little late in the day.

I got home eventually and the election came and went. Afterwards, though, I could see that I was losing weight and realised that eating was becoming unsustainably difficult. I phoned Kaz Mochlinski, a medical oncologist at the Marsden specialising in gastro-intestinal cancers, and a great supporter of mine. He immediately brought me in for tests.

I had a CT scan. It appeared to be clear and I relaxed. But when I went in to see David Cunningham he was clearly not comfortable. He said that notionally the scan was good, and that the radiologist had signed it off as free of cancer, but his face displayed concern. He sat there for a long while, staring at a split screen: on one side the image showed my oesophagus from the scan in June, the other the scan I had just had; he flipped from one image to another. He said there was no evidence of cancer but I should have more tests.

I had a PET scan and then another endoscopy from a Dr Benson, who was perky and confident, saying just before he put me under that he was pretty sure it was not cancer.

When I came round everything had changed.

There is something there, Dr Benson said, but he could not be sure it was a tumour. It was pretty clear, though, that he thought the cancer had returned. He had taken a biopsy, which would decide it one way or another.

A couple of days later, on 9 June, Kaz called and said that the biopsy had shown evidence of cancer cells. He was optimistic as always and said it could be fixed, perhaps by very early surgery, but I knew I had crossed some kind of line, that I had moved to another, more dangerous place.

I accepted this with the kind of calmness I often feel when getting bad news: I hear it but I don't, and I am always looking for a way of turning negative into positive. But this time it was harder. I was not depressed, or in despair, or even deflated. Just shocked.

David Cunningham phoned and was inspirational. He said he was so sorry, he was totally convinced that I had made it through, and that local recurrence of this sort almost never happened so late, with my cancer and treatment profile. He would fight with me every inch of the way and would not let me down. In that call he showed his character and his strength, and he transformed my mood. Murray Brennan called from New York and said I was the last person in whom he had expected to see recurrence. He was shocked, he said. None the less, two years and four months after my original diagnosis, my cancer had returned.

Recurrence is a very different thing from the original diagnosis.

My immediate response to being told I had cancer had been that I would battle through and win. I had a vision of a dark road leading to a light. This framed my entire response to the disease. But the diagnosis of recurrence had a very different effect on me – the road ahead just collapsed, and I was left effectively with nothing, just the kind of fuzzy picture you get if your television stops working.

It was as if my brain and my feelings had a kind of

shared malfunction. And it was to get worse as test after test went the wrong way. The DNA of my life was being unravelled. I was used to fighting hard and getting through, used to being optimistic and having that optimism rewarded, but now the opposite was happening. I was determined to fight, but how?

We went down to the Royal Marsden site in Sutton on 10 June and saw David Cunningham. He looked concerned. I had had a PET scan a couple of days earlier and the findings obviously troubled him. The tumour was big and growing and we had to act fast.

This was a turnaround. I had had a mental image of a couple of stray cancer cells floating around my gullet, not some out-of-control tumour working its way up my throat like a malignant alien. David suggested a possible treatment programme, starting with chemotherapy, going through surgery, and then continuing with more chemotherapy and on to radiation.

The reality of my situation lit up before me: I was going to have to do the whole thing again – but this time, as David kindly pointed out, with an extreme operation not a moderate one, with radiation as well as chemotherapy, and with a much, much smaller chance of survival.

Although I had avoided radical surgery in round one, I would now have to face it in round two, when my reserves were so much lower. It was as if the gods were punishing me for an initial failure of nerve.

It was apparent that David's plan was less a route map forward, more a best guess about what to do. He wrote it down on a scrap of paper, which at least gave it some measure of credibility. But the truth was we were all flying blind. If the cancer had spread I could make no progress. If the tumour was not reduced by chemotherapy then I could not continue, and even then surgery would be incredibly difficult and simply might not be possible.

For all that, however, David had given me hope, and hope was what I wanted. Things may not have been great but at least I had my scrap of paper. The road was coming back.

There was no time to lose. This was Thursday and the chemotherapy was to start on Tuesday. The speed of this response was impressive but it was also alarming. The cancer had to be stopped.

The chemotherapy protocol was different this time, because David feared that the cancer was becoming immune to the drugs that had been used before. He said my swallowing would get better; that it had to get better, as this would be evidence that the tumour was regressing. The idea was that if possible the cancer would shrink almost to nothing.

David's explanation betrayed his anxiety. Every time I contacted the hospital during the treatment they would ask me about my swallowing. And it simply was not getting better. I could feel the tumour now and it seemed to be growing, like a slug in my throat. It was certainly becoming increasingly painful.

After two sessions, David stopped the first chemo and ordered a PET scan. Kaz called, asking me to see David, and I knew all was not well. Essentially the cancerous activity had decreased but the tumour had not changed size. They said this was no problem but immediately changed back to my original chemotherapy protocol, EOX. Once again I was asked a dozen times about my swallowing, which was clearly not improving. After just one session David ordered another PET scan but the results were the same: cancerous activity was down but not the size of the tumour.

David said there was nothing for it but surgery. There was no certainty that this was possible, but if it could be done, it had to be done quickly. I had the impression that unless it could be stopped in its tracks, the tumour was about to make its final decisive move.

I had dinner with Tony Blair. I was not so much low as lost; I could see no way through. Why had it happened? The first diagnosis I understood: I got cancer as others did and I fought it, with as much determination as I could muster. I had taken every pill, undergone every treatment, done everything required of me, got through the crucial two-year mark and still it had returned. Why had it come back?

Tony paused for a second and said slowly: 'Because the cancer has not finished; it is simply not done with you, it wanted more. You may have changed but not by enough, now you have to go on to a higher spiritual level still. You have to use this recurrence to find your real purpose in life.'

Tony was right. I had to find meaning in this recurrence, had finally to come to terms with the purpose of the cancer.

Meanwhile a sub-plot was emerging. People at the Marsden were starting to say that this kind of recurrence only happens when there are issues with the original surgery. That this was the reason the recurrence was localised in this unusual way.

I arranged a conference call between Murray Brennan, who had performed the surgery, Gail and me. I expected him to knock any possibility of surgical problems out of the park with his normal self-assurance. But he did no such thing. With some courage he said that he believed he may have adopted the wrong strategy with the surgery, and as a consequence had left too much of the stomach in, where he now believed the cancer cells may have lain dormant.

He was saying he had not been radical enough.

I took this well, and admired his honesty. Gail just issued a quiet, guttural groan, not of sadness but of suppressed rage at the unfairness of it all.

Gail is never at her most relaxed when hearing bad

news, especially when its cause was in some way avoidable. In effect the British surgeons had been right: radical was best. But this could be said only with hindsight. The decision had been taken totally on its merits and the responsibility was all mine.

Later I talked to Murray about the surgery, reminding him that he was and is a great surgeon, and that sometimes things just do not work out. That is in the nature of life.

Murray called me at every stage to offer support and encouragement. He stayed on the pitch for the whole game. He is an admirable person.

David Cunningham was not giving up. He suggested Professor Mike Griffin at Newcastle's Royal Victoria Infirmary. Mike had established the Northern Oesophago-Gastric Cancer Unit, the largest oesophageal unit not just in the UK but in Europe. David believed that Mike was pretty much the best oesophageal surgeon in the world at the moment, and that he was at the peak of his form. Mike would tell me honestly and objectively if surgery was possible. I should go up to Newcastle just as soon as I could.

I phoned Murray Brennan. He said that he knew Mike Griffin well, had been to his unit more than once, and that he was probably the best person anywhere to do this surgery. He also said that he would have been the ideal person to have performed the original surgery, and blamed himself for not recommending it.

It was not his fault, of course. In dozens and dozens of conversations with senior representatives of the NHS and beyond, no one had mentioned Mike Griffin or Newcastle to us. Alan Milburn, who was always caring and considerate towards me, later conducted some research, spending a whole morning on the internet trying to find whether a normal cancer patient could connect either to Mike Griffin's oesophageal unit or indeed to any other specialist oesophagus unit, but he failed. From a London perspective at least, Mike's unit was in a kind of information black hole.

That night I phoned Mike Griffin and immediately took against him. I had grown used to relaxed, intimate conversations with consultants in which pretty much everything was conducted with a kind of casual equality.

Mike was having none of that. He made it clear that he would be making the decisions, not me, that there was absolutely no certainty that the operation could be carried out, that this was the NHS and that he was in charge. There would be a week of tests, then a team meeting to decide what treatment was appropriate. He just took the situation over.

I did not like this at all. I wanted the operation to go ahead whatever the tests said, and I certainly was not prepared to cede control to anyone.

I arrived in Newcastle on 21 September 2010. It was a very different journey's end this time. Kennedy Airport in

New York was one thing, Newcastle Central Station quite another. My train arrived beneath a Victorian edifice held together by huge arched spans, the essence of a British railway station.

I took a taxi to the hotel where I was to spend my nights, a large, impersonal building overlooking the Tyne, although with amazing views of a clearly transformed city. Newcastle might not quite be New York, but it still had power of its own.

Far too early the next day, I took another taxi through the drizzle to reach the Royal Victoria Infirmary, a stone's throw from the Newcastle United football stadium, St James' Park.

I was stationed for the week in a tiny little ward not far from the oesophageal unit. It comprised just five cubicles, and most of the others were empty. The nurses could not have been friendlier. I had some basic tests and then lay on my bed and waited.

Mike Griffin came in and I immediately realised that I had misjudged him. He was dressed in his scrubs and exuded confidence and authority, his presence immediately making me feel safe. He sat down on the bed and was disconcertingly direct. My position was very serious, only surgery could save me, he said, but there was no guarantee at all that I could have it.

The tests would be taken and at the end of the week my case would be debated at a team meeting. It was not just his decision but the team's. He was very tough, but his toughness was reassuring.

He had gone to school at Fettes where he was a contemporary of Tony Blair, although my long association with Tony was not in his view necessarily a mark in my favour. He had played rugby for Scotland, moved into medicine and then decided that oesophageal cancer was his life. He had looked for somewhere to set up his unit, decided on Newcastle and then built up the largest and probably the best centre of its kind anywhere in the world.

He worked seven days a week, usually starting at half-past six in the morning and finishing at ten or so at night. He never stopped, seeing all his patients twice a day, sometimes more. He instinctively distrusted southerners, New Labour and private medicine, which meant I had a lot of ground to make up.

I completed the week of tests, culminating in an endoscopy which he performed himself. Later that evening he came in to see me, and I felt that in some way I had won him round.

He could not say for sure if the surgery would go ahead, but he was prepared to say there was nothing in the endoscopy that would stop it happening. He was giving me a very faint green light. Then we chatted about cancer and life and I started to talk – typically – about my cancer journey.

He stopped me dead in my tracks, looked me in the eye, and said the one mistake I had made was leaving the NHS. If I had stayed inside it, I would not be in this position today. I argued back, explaining my particular circumstances, but it was all humbug to him. I had left the NHS and I had blown it. He loved the NHS, and he believed that what made it work and what made it special was a commitment to public service that transcended private interest.

He was uneasy about private medicine, particularly in the treatment of cancer, believing it to be corrosive and distortive of clinical priorities. I do not believe he is right, but there is truth in his argument: there is an extraordinary spirit of public service at the absolute heart of the NHS, which is why people value it.

But even Mike was not totally closed-minded on all of this.

He knew Murray Brennan well and admired him, and thought Memorial Sloan-Kettering a remarkable hospital. But he believed that in the end, when it comes to health, private means bad.

In this he was my polar opposite. He was happy and comfortable with private schools, while I am not; he was sceptical of private medicine, while I am much more open to it. Perhaps it was because his father was a reputed surgeon in the NHS and my parents were both teachers in state schools. But he was right about me, I would have been better to have stayed in the NHS.

If only I had listened to Georgia.

The next morning Gail came up and we waited nervously for Mike's verdict. I was more optimistic because of our meeting the night before, but after so much bad news my capacity for hope had withered somewhat.

Mike immediately made it clear that the operation was possible. Even if surgery was successful, however, I had only a 25 per cent chance of five-year survival. And there was a 30 per cent chance that they would start the operation and not be able to finish it because the tumour could not be removed, which to me was a horrible prospect.

There was about the same risk of removing the tumour and not being able to reconstruct my oesophagus, which meant I would have to have some kind of feeding tube in my throat. This did not seem to worry Gail, who just wanted me alive, tube or not.

A second operation of this sort was taking me into unknown waters. It would be much tougher than the first and there was no way of predicting how difficult it would be, nor in all honesty its impact on my quality of life.

I asked how long I would live if I did not have the surgery. Mike replied: six months to a year. He asked what my decision was: did I want the surgery or not? It was a stupid question; of course I wanted the surgery. I had fought for it for months and now it was going to happen. I did not mind if I walked around with a tube in my neck, I wanted life. He gave me a date – 26 October – and we went home, happy.

*

I used the intervening period as best I could, spending a lot of time with my daughters, going on trips with both, and to Venice again with Gail. Grace stayed with me for much of the time, which was wonderful. Georgia was always around. I got as fit as I could, rewrote my letters to my family, and went once again to see the vicar about the funeral. This time I was stronger but sadder. I did not want to leave my family, and especially not my wife.

On the Friday before the operation, Tony came to see me, just as he had on the eve of my previous surgery. He said one of his most precious possessions was a sixth-century ring from Mount Sinai. He gave it to me for luck. I was touched but anxious, certain that I would lose it. I lose things very easily.

I travelled to Newcastle with Gail on Saturday 23 October and arrived at our flat, which was modern and flash, like something out of *Footballers' Wives*. It was in the heart of the city and you could see and hear the nightlife. Nothing, not rain or gale force winds or severe snow, stops Newcastle kids from going out at night and having fun. But they were all so friendly, it was impossible not to love it there.

That night we joined in and had dinner surrounded by a crowd of incredibly glamorous-looking young people, easily forty years younger than me. We walked back through the cold, picking our way through students using the pavement as a temporary bed.

The night went well. By now we were old hands at

pre-surgery sleeping. The next day we arrived at the oesophageal unit – Ward 36 – exactly on time, as though punctuality would in some way increase my chances.

I was put in a reasonably sized cubicle with a television and a little shower room. And then we waited as a stream of clinicians explained to me how dire my immediate future looked.

This is Mike Griffin's way: to be totally honest and totally explicit about bad news. One after another they came in: the excellent anaesthetist, Conor Gillan, who said an epidural was the preferred method of pain relief, and that it should work, but might not; Rachel, an outstanding specialist nurse who said it would be tougher than perhaps I thought; and then a representative from the intensive care unit, who said it would be like a kind of torture: deprived of sleep and food for at least a week.

And in the middle of this Mike dropped in, clearly anxious, making it plain that there was a serious chance that the operation would have to be aborted after it had begun. I shared his fear; I hated the thought of waking up to failure.

By the end of the day, I was drained of energy and emotion and Gail had just had too much. We were battered into submission. Mike came one last time, saw Gail and moved to reassure her. When she left I felt lonely. I slept a little but woke often, hoping the morning would come slowly.

Gail arrived at six, and with incredible strength had

recovered all her poise. And then we started an absurd domestic row. I, like a fool, had been drinking water during the night, and a nurse had said this might be a problem for the surgery. Gail simply could not believe I was capable of such complete stupidity. But the bickering got us through the next hour.

Then Mike came in, exuding an aura of confidence that completely calmed us down. There were no doubts now, no worries about an aborted operation; he had risen to the moment.

At 8 a.m. they came for me, and for the second time in two years I left Gail for a serious operation. I walked through the corridors leading to the operating theatre with an equal mixture of fear and excitement. There was no escape now. I had to do it, and although I was scared, I was also resolute. I was up for it.

The Bottom of a Murky Sea

I walked into the small pre-surgery room where Conor, the anaesthetist, would administer the epidural. Starting to feel anxious, I held on to the excitement and the determination that was driving me through. But I felt the surgery coming towards me like an express train. There were only moments left.

Courage is supposed to be grace under pressure, but it is really composure in the face of inevitability, being strong not just when the odds favour you, but when they most decidedly do not.

Conor did well with the epidural, but struggled with the boniness of my back and my evident anxiety. At one point he jammed the needle into a rib and the pain was excruciating. I was starting to unravel, but somehow he finished the procedure and then, thankfully, all went blank.

Gail, meanwhile, had to endure another desperate vigil, waiting almost twenty-four hours for me to come round. From the start people were calling and texting, anxious and concerned. But they knew that no news was good news and that the longer the operation went on, the better.

Hour followed hour. After five hours or so Gail went for a walk and bumped into Mike as he took a break. He told her the surgery on the stomach had gone well, and now they had to turn me over and break through into the chest. It was clear that the operation would not now be aborted.

Five hours later, Mike emerged again and told Gail that while the operation had been difficult it had been a complete success. She rushed in to see me. I looked, she said, far more dead than alive, but she sent out an email to all my friends saying that Mike had performed a miracle.

Because of the severity of the surgery they kept me sedated and breathing through a ventilator all night. Gail was struck by the way that the intensive care staff watched me, unwaveringly vigilant. At about six they decided to slowly wake me. I came round in a way distinctively different from my New York experience.

Then I had awoken to a bright light almost full in my

face. I remember feeling close to the sun. This time it was as if I was at the bottom of a murky sea, the light far above me, subdued, distant, swirling with the waves.

Gradually the light got closer and I heard sounds. Immediately a voice said: 'It's over, the surgery has been a complete success.' In a second I was calm.

Then I felt the ventilating tube in my throat, vast and obtrusive. I started to cough, feeling spasms of unbearable pain in my throat where the ventilator met my wound. The more I coughed the worse the pain, and then it became intolerable, just beyond description.

My heart rate shot up and the pain, the panic and the sense of suffocation combined to produce a moment of complete blackness. I knew this was the biggest test of my life, one that I was not certain I could pass.

I did not feel alone, though. The pain somehow connected to the suffering of others in the world. At this crucial moment I felt not isolation but empathy, some kind of recognition of the power of the human spirit.

I used every resource I had to control the pain. I tried meditating but it made no difference at all. I attempted to pray but could not get a foothold. The pain and panic just rose. And then I thought of Gail. If she could tough it out through the day and the night, then so could I.

And that was enough. I was able to hang on until they pulled out the ventilator. The moment had passed, I had got through it. Just.

*

I saw as if through a watery lens that Gail had arrived at my side. I could not talk, I had tubes everywhere, I must have looked ghastly. She was nervous, anxious, tired, but vibrant with hope and love. She said one thing over and over again: you have made it.

And then, to gain some peace, I held up my finger to indicate quiet. Gail looked at my raised finger and saw it instead as a demand. 'He wants something, but what is it?' The nurses gathered round to try to find out. Ungratefully, I slumped back, thinking: why does no one understand me? But this note of domestic disharmony was a small comfort too.

As my vision slowly returned I was able to make some sense of the space in which I now found myself. I was surrounded by instruments, tubes and nurses. There were twelve beds, with a central supervision area. As I looked I saw the contrast between the brightness of the intensive care unit and the darkness around me. My neighbours included not only seriously ill people moving towards recovery after their operations, but others in a state of grave illness, fighting off death, kept alive by medical science and impressively dedicated care.

One man had serious pneumonia and lay there unable to speak at all or move much, in a kind of permanent limbo of suffering. Another had endured a major stroke and groaned constantly day and night. One day one of the patients was in such emotional and physical pain that he indicated he wanted to end his life. A friend sat by his bed and prayed.

I had never been so close to pain, death and severe suffering before. It affected Gail greatly, making her feel that life hung by a thread, that the path you walked in apparent security was in fact treacherous. It affected the medical staff too, especially the younger ones. Sucked so close to death, they had to find a way of dealing with it. They wanted to talk about it: what did it mean, what could and should they do about it?

There were moments of hope and mystery. On my second day in intensive care, one of the patients was visited by his sister and his wife. They sat down – one elderly and white-haired, the other middle-aged and sprightly – and started to sing, not quietly and privately but loudly and confidently. Without warning, the haunting cadence of 'Danny Boy' filled the room. And then a remarkable thing happened. Everyone in the room stopped what they were doing, turned to the singers and froze, trapped in a moment somewhere between the real and the ethereal. And they stayed there, unmoving, until the voices fell silent five or six songs later. It was as if time had stood still, replaced by the sublime.

And there were moments of farce too. Gradually my production of urine started to decline. Every hour it got worse. The doctors thought at first it was because I was not drinking enough. Gradually they worked their way to the truth, which I had long since suspected, that my catheter had stopped working and they would need to replace it. This was a frightening prospect; I was certain that it would be painful.

The curtains were closed around me and a small medical crowd appeared. I felt my misfortune was a spectator sport. The surgeon was in control and took the old catheter out, which was not painful at all.

I felt it was going my way, but then he produced a large white sheet about a metre across with a hole about an inch wide in its centre, which was placed over me. I don't think I have ever felt quite so exposed. The sister produced a calliper-like instrument and measured me. And then in a completely surreal moment she said: 'I think we need a small bore tube; it's not very big, is it?'

She was referring, I hope, to the size of the aperture and nothing else, but it was still embarrassing. The crowd was asked to leave and it was me and the surgeon. He injected a local anaesthetic, which amazingly did not hurt, and inserted the new catheter, causing me almost no pain at all. Not for the first time, my fear had been misplaced.

For most of the time I lay there in a kind of limbo, not able to talk much, but able to hear everything. It became clear to me that nurses – and doctors – assume that a patient's consciousness disappears if their eyes are shut; with your eyes closed, you would be talked about as if you were not there. This was understandable but disquieting. It was also interesting: I would lie there, not asleep yet not really awake, constantly and unavoidably listening. The first morning a doctor reviewed my surgery to his team, going through detail after grisly detail, totally oblivious to the fact that I could hear every word. I had moved in the blink of an eye from being a subject to an object.

Time after time, comments made to my face were flatly contradicted by remarks made just seconds later when I appeared to be asleep. One moment a nurse told me I could have as much pain relief as I wanted, but the second my eyes were shut he turned to his companion and said, 'He's obviously neurotic about pain, and the more pain relief he gets the more he'll want.'

Completely true, of course. Pain was an issue for me, certainly. I felt low-level pain almost continuously and acute pain quite often, and I hated it. I learnt the disabling power of pain, how hard it is to cope with, how undermining it can be. The Geordies were stoic, they toughed it out and got through it. In contrast, I felt like a hopeless southern wimp.

The worst moments – in Newcastle, as in New York – were when they changed my position in bed. This always caused pain to shoot through my body like a small electric shock. With pain, as with almost everything else in cancer, the fear is worse than the reality, and every time you are able to defeat it your body and spirit become stronger. I still hate pain but I can now tolerate it in ways unimaginable three years ago. But I do now feel a greatly heightened empathy with anyone suffering serious pain. Cancer does change you like that.

The nurses in the unit were strong, opinionated and forceful. They would chatter constantly, often focusing on financial pressures, complaining about such matters as Wayne Rooney and his salary, which was an issue at the time. It seemed clear to me that excessive differentials in pay were straining the public-service spirit. It is hard not to feel sympathy. These nurses were working twelve-hour shifts with critically ill patients, on the very cusp of life and death, and yet they were paid £33,000 or so a year, not £180,000 a week.

The days may have been interesting but the nights were challenging. There was no protection at all, no comfort zone of sleeping pills or tranquillisers, no alcohol, no talking to friends or partners.

At night you are completely exposed, there is no hiding place. I had three drains, a feeding tube, a tube up my nose, an oxygen mask around my face, and much more besides. My whole body was aching and I could barely move. As night arrived I was placed semi-upright, and just sat there, trapped in the same fixed position. Hour after hour passed as I lay there, dozing at best for an hour or so, until at last dawn arrived, bringing with it the 5.30 round of tests.

The first night was the worst – I do not think I slept even for a moment, my heart beating rapidly and panic always just below the surface. I was fearful that I would not have the courage or capacity to get through.

That night and the one that followed were also made harder by the constant hallucinations. Even without morphine, my mind became difficult to control. Shutting my eyes would produce strange and inexplicable patterns floating inside my head. These moved in a constant swirling flux, making me feel more secure with my eyes open than shut. At first these patterns were black, then gradually they changed to white and then to colour, but still they were disturbing, nothing was ever solid.

After my epidural failed and I began taking morphine it got worse. I became trapped in living nightmares, unable to speak, move or raise an alarm. My bed seemed never to stay in the same place but would move around, creating new perspectives, new angles, new dimensions.

Throughout my life I have always trusted my mind never to let me down, but here I lost control of it, overwhelmed by the drugs and the tiredness. After a while I refused to take morphine, preferring physical pain to mental distress.

After two days in intensive care I returned to Ward 36, and was given a bed in the critical care unit. It was like coming home. The nurses all knew me by name and it felt so safe. I was soon institutionalised, settling into a standard routine.

I was woken by a nurse at half-past five or so and given tests, and then moved to a chair. For the first few days I was washed, and then sat there bereft of energy until Louise and the other physiotherapists arrived.

Before long I could walk the corridors of the hospital just as I had done in New York. But here, unlike New York, people smiled and the mood was jocular, the patients bracing themselves to be cheerful through the pain. It was very British.

After the walk I would sit on my bed reading about a page an hour and wait for a visitor, invariably Gail in those early days. At first we laughed a lot, and it really did feel good to be alive, but after a while I was a less attractive patient. Gail was a saint for putting up with me.

In the evenings I read and watched television, staying up late, delaying the night for as long as I possibly could. The days were slow but they were passing. Alastair Campbell came up, bringing with him Brendan Foster, the athlete and BBC commentator. Brendan exemplifies the North-East: big-hearted, generous in spirit, protective and proud of his region.

One of the purposes of the visit was for Alastair to meet Mike Griffin, always a risk given Mike's wariness not just of New Labour but also of spin. In the end it worked. Initially, they eyed each other with a kind of territorial suspicion, but soon they became involved in a two-person *Question of Sport*, trading increasingly inconsequential and obscure facts about irrelevant sporting events. After about half an hour honour was satisfied and they became friends. Grace and Brendan looked on, bemused.

All the staff were outstanding. Mike would visit at least twice a day, at seven in the morning and then later at

perhaps seven in the evening, his presence calming everyone. He had a wonderful touch with patients, treating
each equally and with genuine respect, and he would
always be there at weekends.

His patients gained, but I am sure his family suffered.
Mike was not the kind of person who understood the
term work–life balance. He was driven: to save lives, to
make his unit the best in the world, to do everything he
possibly could for his patients. He could be stubborn and
was not easily open to compromise. But that was at the
core of his strength.

If you started an argument with Mike it would take a
very long time to finish, and you never quite felt that you
had won. We spent hours in the evenings discussing politics and life.

The nurses were exemplary, never once failing to be
positive or professional. At first they were a blur of uniforms and Geordie accents but gradually they emerged as
individuals, with strong and sometimes angular personal-
ities. They may initially have been suspicious of me, but
gradually relationships formed – during a twelve-hour shift
you get to know somebody and they get to know you.
They would always start their shift full of energy and
always leave tired. You could see the strain and the responsibility taking hold as the time went on. Twelve hours on
your feet is a long time.

They were impeccable; it is impossible to imagine
receiving better care. This was a team, a unit, in every

sense of the word, working together almost intuitively, led ultimately by Mike but with everyone willing to step up and take responsibility when it mattered. It was impressive.

After a while Georgia replaced Gail. Georgia loved Newcastle, the hospital and Mike, seeing them as the embodiment of her values, something to believe in. It was completely her kind of place.

The week ground on with nothing getting much better; although not impossible, it was a slog. Like everybody else I was getting through. But the surgery and its aftermath had brought me closer to pain and death. I felt that when the crucial moment had come my faith could not get me through. I felt deserted by it, and that I had deserted it in turn. A priest came by, sent by my local church, ironically at a time when I was suffering pretty intense discomfort. We talked about pain, faith and doubt and I could see my faith settling into a new place, more sceptical and doubting, more aligned to my personality.

After ten days I moved into a room on my own, and then I collapsed with tiredness. Alistair Gascoigne, the man in charge of both the intensive care and the infectious diseases units, happened to spot me in the corridor and thought at once I was not well.

Alistair is another of those NHS giants. Brutally funny, he was brilliant at getting seriously ill patients to lift their moods. He was more subversive than Mike, more acerbic but also more private. Like Mike he started at some ungodly hour, working till late and most weekends. He entered rooms quietly, almost unnoticed, and had a sixth sense for the condition of his patients.

He immediately suspected I had an infection and, on a Saturday, personally pushed me in a wheelchair to the radiology department for an X-ray, hovering there all day. By mid-afternoon he had seen enough and said we would have to put in a drain.

This meant using radiology to plot a course from my back to my lungs, and then shoving in a tube that could drain off infected fluid. It sounded unpleasant but was actually not too bad, and luckily Grace was there to hold my hand. Eventually the tube was in and liquid flooded out, about two litres of it. This in just a day or so. Infections flare up in hours. Within days I would have been in trouble. In the event, the infection was killed off by a massive dose of antibiotics that was to last for four weeks.

Alistair's intervention strikes me as amazing; he showed almost mystical powers in diagnosing me. He would visit every day for the rest of my stay to check I was all right, and we talked about our daughters, living in Newcastle, and the long walks he took on the Northumbrian beaches with his dog. He was reflective and modest, his low-key demeanour a stark contrast to his enormous importance to the hospital.

After exactly three weeks, and exactly according to Mike's plan, I left the hospital and went to the flat in Newcastle where I was to stay for another month. The snows came and lay a foot or so deep on the streets, making walking hard but the views beautiful. There are worse places to be than Newcastle at Christmas time.

Towards the end of December came the histology meeting. This is the report of the forensic examination of the tissues that determines your prognosis.

On one level I was optimistic about it. I believed that having gone through all this treatment, I would be OK, and I did not see how the pre-testing would have missed the spread of cancer. But on another I was uneasy. In medicine – like politics – good news travels fast. I was aware that the report would have been available for a while and I felt no indications at all that it was positive.

Mostly, though, both Gail and I were so numbed that we were almost beyond caring. The last eight weeks had been traumatic and this was perhaps the twentieth time we had arrived for one of these life or death meetings. We were exhausted.

The Unfinished Life

We arrived at the hospital and met Sarah, Mike's deputy consultant, on her way out. She was warm enough but seemed distant, and I felt an intimation that all might not be well. We sat in the waiting room and the meeting was an hour late in starting, something else that did not feel right.

Mike came in with Claire, a specialist nurse I had become close to. He started with a rather abstract discussion of my general condition, how I felt, how my feeding was going, what my symptoms were. This was not going well: good news always comes early in these meetings, it's not left to the end. And he was low, his normal sparkle missing.

Then he said, 'Let's move on to the histology.' He said

the margins were good although tight, the tumour had been removed, but the cancer had been more prevalent than expected, had taken hold more deeply. Seven of the twenty-three lymph nodes extracted had been contaminated with cancer.

Seven.

I felt slightly sick. I knew this was very, very bad.

He said there was a very high chance that the cancer would come back. I asked what my chances were: still 25 per cent? No, he said, more like 20 per cent, but he looked to the ground and rather mumbled as he spoke, obviously not really believing it. If I took chemoradiotherapy then that might add another 10 to 15 per cent, but again he did not say this with great conviction.

I turned and looked him straight in the eye. 'Is it going to come back?' I asked. 'Yes,' he said, 'it is likely that it will.'

By now the mood in the room was becoming dark. Mike was low, Claire subdued and Gail shell-shocked. I did my best to lift spirits, but failed. We left.

'That didn't go so well,' I said to Gail. 'No, not perfectly,' she said. We walked on, knowing the future had changed once more.

I told the kids honestly that the prognosis was not good.

A few days later Gail left. Georgia came up and we went to a discharge meeting with Mike. This time our mood had lifted and we were pretty buoyant. Mike told

Georgia the unvarnished truth about my situation, and she took it well, seduced in part by the positivity of our shared mood.

A couple of days afterwards Georgia and I went to a coffee morning that Mike and Claire organise each year. We expected to find twenty people sitting around chatting in a side room somewhere. In fact, eight hundred people turned up, completely filling the Newcastle Civic Centre.

Eight hundred people whose lives had been touched by Mike and his team.

The longest surviving patient had had his operation performed twenty years ago, just a few years after the unit started. It was as if Mike could see the whole of his life's work in front of him. If only politics could be so unambiguously virtuous.

We sat at a table with a group of cancer survivors from South Shields. They were warm and direct, tolerating no nonsense. They immediately took me in hand. We talked about what cancer meant to them. And it was, in essence, what it had meant to me: finding a way to deal with the fears of the night; the importance of community and collective support; the need to be positive and optimistic. Above all was the recognition that cancer is cruel, but it also has the power to change people's lives. It had obviously changed theirs.

They had set up an oesophageal cancer self-help group in South Shields that met in a pub once a week, and had an outreach programme for other cancer survivors. They invited me to visit, and I said one day I hope I will. Although miles apart geographically, we shared the same perceptions of cancer and how to fight it. I felt part of a shared journey.

We spent Christmas out of London in the snow. Just us and the kids. There was no hiding here, we all knew the situation. The family was under strain but we were close.

Georgia had taken the original diagnosis hard, and tended not to want to discuss my cancer with me. She had just wanted to be happy and positive and helpful, and seemed to feel that any sign of sadness would betray her anxiety. The problem was too deep to discuss. But Newcastle had released her. Now she accepted cancer and the reality of my situation, and could openly face and talk about it.

Grace was different – only too happy to talk about the cancer, wanting facts not flim-flam: she wanted data, actual percentages, real lengths of time. And, consummate at black humour, she could joke about it. She talked about it all openly from the start. I think, though, that she was set back by the recurrence; it was not something she had thought would happen.

I hoped and believed that my relationship with my children was deepening all the time. We implicitly decided to bring the future forward, to compress ten years or so into one.

The kids sucked me dry. Georgia wanted to know all about the way I thought. How did I develop a concept? What were my values? Why did I believe what I believed? Grace wanted hard, usable, practical advice. At one stage she asked me to write down every likely eventuality that might befall her, and supply a satisfactory answer. Facing the possibility of my departure, she wanted a handbook for life.

With the children all this was in a way easier than it might have been. It is in the nature of things that children outlive their parents. There is a point of natural parting.

For Gail it was different. She did not want intensity, or purpose, or accelerated living, she wanted quiet and normality – not the future brought forward but the present extended. She had always envisaged a future free from work where we would just potter around, grow old as companions.

We had known each other so long that we had created a kind of shared world. After her husband died, Katharine Whitehorn wrote: 'Marriage is the water in which you swim, the land you live in, the habits, the assumptions you share.' Pottering around in later life seems the easiest thing to achieve. But now it was something I simply could not guarantee. This was the hardest thing to bear, and it does not get much easier.

In London we went to see David Cunningham. Gail had with her Mike's discharge report, which she had been

discreetly keeping from me. I grabbed it and read it, seeing
his crucial summation: 'Philip Gould has a very poor prognosis . . . The patient is aware he has only a slim chance of
a cure.' Hearing this is one thing, reading it quite another.
I felt chilled.

We went in to see David, who was as always positive
but never dishonest. He said the next step would be
chemo-radiation, which would last six weeks and would
involve radiation on a daily basis except weekends. Later
we would explore genetic and DNA diagnosis, to see if
some kind of experimental cure might be possible in the
event of recurrence.

I felt hope but I had been winded.

I was keen to get on with the radiotherapy, but by now
eating had become very difficult for me again and my
swallowing pains were worsening. David sent me off to a
consultant called Jervoise Andreyev, who deals particularly
with the symptoms of radiotherapy linked to surgery. He
was brilliant, a typical Marsden hidden gem. He prescribed
a whole new world of drugs and within days my symptoms were becoming manageable. But Mike phoned to say
that I simply would not get through the treatment without a feeding tube, because I would not be able to eat in
the middle of it.

So the next day I returned to Newcastle to have a feeding tube fitted and was reunited with the team, who
seemed genuinely pleased to see me. After the surgery

Mike came down and we talked about the harsh reality of my prognosis. Mike believes that it is right to tell the unvarnished truth and to tell the whole family at the same time; it stops a sense of grievance and unfairness festering.

I said there was another, deeper reason for telling the whole family the truth. It is that with the knowledge of your likely early death, you can reconfigure time, use it on your own terms. In truth, having an idea of the likely timescale of your life is a privilege not available to many. It is so much better than a sudden death, with no time to prepare.

I did not like radiotherapy, much to the chagrin of my consultant, Diana Tait. She kept telling me that this was the Year of Radiotherapy: could I not enjoy it a little more? She was terrific and so were her staff, but I found radiotherapy to be among the few things in cancer that lowered my mood.

The very first time I went into the radiotherapy unit I sensed a gloom among the patients waiting to be treated, a mood quite different in character from that of patients waiting for surgery and chemotherapy. This is not because radiotherapy is particularly unpleasant or painful. It is not. It just has a kind of dulling effect, and even as I write this I feel the ghosts of the experience returning.

The treatment itself is straightforward. You just lie under a huge rotating machine with a name like a battle-ship: mine was called Joford. The machine chugs round, blasting its rays from four different angles. There is no pain, in fact no sensation at all except the buzzing of the machine while the X-rays are going through. The only discomfort is lying for a few minutes at full stretch, unable to move, with your arms above your head. I played music on an iPod and it passed in a trice. But no one enjoys it much, and some seem to struggle.

One day I saw a man standing uneasily, unable to sit because of the pain. Another was being sick in the bathroom. A third was sobbing quietly. I think this was probably a reflection of their state of illness rather than the treatment, but it took a while to grow used to it.

For many radiotherapy is much less traumatic than this, and it may just have been the patient cohort I was in. But the patients never lost their resolve. They kept going, day after day, getting through it, though some were obviously approaching their last stages.

The point of the radiotherapy was to sterilise the immediate region of surgery and the wider area around it in which the contaminated lymph nodes were found. It was entirely about stopping localised recurrence. The problem was that as a result of the surgery I had undergone, the remaining shreds of my oesophagus and stomach were clustered in an area very close to my heart and lungs, so it was tricky to find a safe path. The full blast of the rays went right through the surgery wound.

Even after day one, I could feel some pain in the wound and it just grew from there. I developed a pretty horrible cough, but that passed and the middle weeks proved not to be too bad. By the last couple of weeks, though, the pain was acute and accompanied by persistent vomiting – not of food, as I was not eating, but of phlegm caused by inflammation. This process of pain and vomiting went on for days.

So my life became the familiar business of grinding on. Four times a day I would take an array of pills, including the crucial chemotherapy medications, and each session of pill-taking would take as long as an hour. At times like this cancer becomes a moment-by-moment endurance test, with nothing for it but to tough things out and seek distraction.

And throughout all this was the saga of the feeding tube. It had been inserted in my stomach, or rather my small intestine, and to feed I had to attach it each night to a pump which would administer a litre and a half of a sweet gooey liquid that purported to be food.

Gail hated this. She hated the noise of the pump and the smell of the liquid and the fact that our private space had become more like a hospital room than a bedroom. Above all, she hated the tube that dangled from my stomach like a plastic eel and was my lifeline. She was certain that I would pull it out, convinced that when this happened I would no longer be able to eat.

Of course, I did pull it out – twice in fact – but a terrific surgeon at UCH managed to get it back in on both occasions. It also exploded once, flooding my T-shirt, my jeans and the floor beneath me with foul-smelling bile.

There was an embarrassed silence in the kitchen as the puddle beneath me gradually grew. This might have been a low point. But I just accepted it and moved on.

Cancer does make you stronger.

The radiotherapy finished and I saw David Cunningham for a post-treatment consultation. Positive as always, he said that things had gone as well as they could have on the long journey that had begun with that first scrap of paper mapping out my treatment seven months before. Everything that had been planned had happened.

We moved to the future and the vast panoply of tests they were now carrying out: DNA, genetics, stem cell, and on and on. These were not to prevent recurrence, but to deal with recurrence if it happened.

The next scan was due in early June, which seemed an eternity away. I unwound, relaxed and did as little as possible, determined this time to do things differently.

The day of the scan arrived. Gail and I were both really nervous, anxiety creeping up on us, growing by the day. Gail called after I had the scan, desperate to know what the findings were. I said I had no idea, but at that moment Kaz called saying all was good. I felt that despite all expectations I had a chance of life. At least for the next six months, until the next scan, we could be free.

I called Gail and she was virtually gasping for air, so surprised that finally we had some good news, so frightened that once again good news would turn to bad. But for now, it was OK.

We went to see David Cunningham, who said the scan was excellent, that this was a significant step forward and that my prognosis had improved a little. Of course the odds were still against me, but I did not care much about that. I had a chance, and a chance was all I needed. The door which had seemed to be closed had opened a little. Life, short or long, lay ahead of me once more.

The Cancer Odyssey

The journey to this point had taken place on many levels, and was one that had changed me in many ways – I hope for the better. I now had a different conception of myself, of cancer, of my politics, of the NHS, of my family and friends, and perhaps above all, of my wife, whom I now appreciate in new and different ways.

Much of this journey had been personal but some of it had been political, not in the party sense but in the way I used different health systems, with different values, in different countries. This was the spine of my journey, taking me from a private clinic and private oncologist in Harley Street to an endowment hospital in New York City, then back to the Royal Marsden, switching again to Newcastle's Royal Victoria Infirmary, while often using the UCH in London.

On my way I must have talked to literally hundreds of doctors, nurses and patients. There were real differences between the systems. In the United States the quality of care at Memorial Sloan-Kettering was outstanding but it was impossible to escape the reality of unequal access, despite the institution's commendable efforts to widen it.

In the British private system the quality of care was impeccable, but access to it was not free and open, and you could not avoid the sense that the real firepower of much of the private sector came from the NHS.

Although both are NHS hospitals, the Marsden and the Royal Victoria have distinctive approaches. The Marsden generates a significant amount of its income from private patients. Newcastle, or at least the Northern Oesophago-Gastric Unit, is pretty much 100 per cent dedicated to the NHS with only the very odd exception (like me, for whom Mike claimed health insurance to fund his admirable cancer campaign).

This does produce differences. In the Marsden there are many shared services like radiotherapy, but also some, like chemotherapy, where private and NHS patients go to different units. Despite this the values of the NHS dominate, and it is very much an NHS hospital. Private and public do work together here. In the Northern Oesophago-Gastric Cancer Unit all services are shared, and all patients treated as if on the NHS, creating a powerful fusion of excellence and equality.

So how did they all compare? The London Clinic offered comfort, speed and little waiting. But so did the Marsden: just as fast, just as comfortable, just as little waiting, and with the knowledge that you were part of an NHS system containing numerous world-class consultants. Similarly, the private oncology was good and Maurice Slevin was excellent. But the Marsden was equally comfortable and convenient, and the consultant who looked after me had developed the protocol for treating oesophageal cancer used by the whole world.

Finally the surgery. It is of course true that Memorial Sloan-Kettering is an outstanding institution, but when it came to my surgery the oesophagus unit in Newcastle was better. The nursing was warm and attentive, the rooms nicer, the physiotherapy and the surgery superb. This is not in any way to belittle Memorial Sloan-Kettering, which is a great hospital, only to show how good was Newcastle.

This does not mean I believe that in health private is bad and the NHS always does better, because I do not. Nor do I believe that it is impossible for a private institution to have public values, because clearly it can − I received good treatment everywhere, private, public and mixed. But I did get my best treatment in NHS hospitals, whether as a private or an NHS patient.

The NHS is not perfect but at its best it can be very good indeed. In many ways I started the journey an NHS sceptic, but finish as an NHS enthusiast. This does not obviate the need for reform, quite the opposite. It was reform – plus funding – that made the modern NHS possible, and as health provision faces constantly shifting challenges, the NHS will always need to adapt.

In the modern world all institutions need to change if they are to flourish, and the NHS is no exception. But from my experience as a patient in the NHS there was little resistance to change. The fight against cancer altered almost daily, something that health practitioners seemed to know instinctively.

The question is, of course, what kind of reform. If I was responsible for reforming the NHS, I would want to be sure of three things: that the system and the people within it were robust enough to survive the change envisaged; that those who work in the NHS were bound into the process that achieved the change; and, finally, that the driving essence of the NHS, its commitment to public service, was not weakened or harmed. That is the most important thing of all.

But important though politics is, it is the personal journey of cancer that really matters. I have learnt that fear can be defeated and, if it is, then human possibility is unlocked; that we are stronger than we think and as we overcome what seems to be an impossible challenge then we get stronger still; that the power of community is limitless and gives us courage we did not know we had; that optimism and hope can help to defeat fear and darkness; that the human spirit within us all is more powerful and more resolute than we can ever imagine; and that although cancer is a terrible disease, it has the capacity to transform us.

This may sound trite, but I believe it to be true. I am not sentimental about this. I know that cancer is a savage and unrelenting disease that strikes down children, young people, mothers and fathers, wives and husbands in ways that are unspeakably cruel and brutal. I know that this brutality is worse when the patient is most isolated, disadvantaged, vulnerable.

I did not write this to praise cancer but to kill it. I want every single person reading these words, if they have symptoms of what may be oesophageal cancer and are too nervous to take the test, to have a check-up tomorrow; I want anyone who can afford it to give money to the charities listed elsewhere in this book. I want cancer over.

But as long as cancer continues, I want people to know that, frightening and challenging as it is, they have the power within themselves to deal with it, and will come out changed and stronger. Cancer can at one and the same time destroy and transform. Why this is, I am not quite sure. Cancer is an iconic illness that seems to live and breathe in the darkest recesses of our fear. Other diseases may be more deadly and more terrible but cancer has a unique power to provoke awe and fear. Yet it is the power of cancer to transform that led Lance Armstrong to write: 'The truth is that cancer was the best thing that ever happened to me. I don't know why I got the illness but it did wonders for me and I would not want to walk away from it. Why would I want to change, even for a day, the most important and shaping thing in my life?'

I would not have chosen cancer but I do not regret it. And certainly I would not have wanted to have died the person that I was before the recurrence. I believe that somehow or other in this second stage of cancer I discovered a sense of purpose that I had never found before.

A few days ago Pete Jones, my closest friend from university, came to see me. His mother is eighty-six, and was that day undergoing the same operation that I had gone through: a full radical oesophageal resection. I had spoken to her a couple of days earlier and she was frightened, but utterly determined. Her courage was inspiring.

I talked with Pete about this, and it was clear that his experience with her, and perhaps with me, had changed him. He had seen the power of cancer, and the transformation it could achieve. He had witnessed his mother reaching out, giving love and showing courage, and seen that a kind of viral collective power had been unlocked.

He had not become religious, but he had discovered the power of the human spirit in facing and defeating adversity. He was caught somewhere between God and man, not believing yet not sceptical, and certain that there was a purpose to it all.

And looking back at what has happened to me, it is difficult not to believe that running through all the extraordinary and unexpected events that occurred was some thread of meaning.

This journey has taken me from London to New York to Newcastle and back to London, and through challenges of fear and pain I thought myself too weak ever to surmount. I may fall at the next hurdle, but for the moment the journey has been inspiring and in truth I would not change much of it.

It is my life, revealed to me. Do whatever you can to avoid cancer, but if you cannot avoid it, be confident that you have the resources to be able to cope with it.

Cancer is an iconic disease, but icons crumble.

The Tall Black Cloud

That test result in June had a disproportionate effect, offering the slightest glimpse of a future. We had no illusions about this; we knew that the cancer would return. But we believed that somehow or other we had gained an island of emotional immunity that stretched from June to December, the date of the next round of tests, a safe house on Planet Cancer.

And so we took a break. Gail wanted a proper holiday, Italian light, blue skies and lovely hotels. She wanted somewhere with no work and no medical intervention and where, after the miserable summer we had had so far in England, there was some sun. 'A chill-out holiday in a very beautiful place' was her plan.

So on Saturday 30 July we flew from Gatwick to Naples

and headed south to Positano on the Amalfi Coast, bound
for a quiet, supportive retreat somewhere between sea and
sky. The beautiful Le Sirenuse, overlooking the village and
the sparkling turquoise waters of the bay, was her choice.
This was a holiday and she was determined we were going
to have it.

And so we did. Day by day we got through. I ate a lot
and once even went swimming. Gail sat by the pool and
read. Sometimes we walked for half an hour in the village.
In the evenings we dined and I did my best to eat
respectable amounts.

But other forces were at work. I had become determined to write down everything I thought I had learnt
and had come to believe as a result of my experiences.

I had written for *The Times* the long series of articles
about the realities of cancer which, in a slightly different
version, form the early part of this narrative. They were
very well received and although I had written them quite
quickly, I think they made a difference. So I decided to go
on telling the story of my cancer odyssey.

But now, like a tall black cloud hanging over the
summer sea I could see from my hotel window, a new
problem presented itself.

I had agreed to update my politics book, *The Unfinished
Revolution*. The new material was supposed to be twenty
pages long. But what I wanted to add turned out to be
more like 140 pages, entailing a very different commitment of time and energy.

Unforgivably, I allowed my work on the book to intrude on the holiday. I would sit in my room, writing furiously, while Gail lay by the pool alone. What Gail had hoped would be a magical, transcendental period of peace was assailed by my almost insatiable desire to write down everything I knew.

I was a new person, but in this respect I felt a bit like an old person in disguise. What I tried to do during that holiday was seize the moment and smell the roses. Whenever Gail and I were together, which was most of the time, we were extraordinarily close. She kept trying to get me to eat. Unable to keep a lot of food down, I had become a very fussy eater, but I liked one speciality of the hotel, strawberries dipped in chocolate. So Gail ordered plates of them, leaving them around our room hoping I would absent-mindedly start eating.

But the conflict between the deadline for the book and my commitment to Gail produced one of the most guilty and unhappy feelings I have had in years. I was caught between breaking a contract and breaking a vow.

After a week we moved north, travelling by train from Naples via Rome to the beautiful coastal town of Orbetello. The journey was a long one, more than four hours, and to Gail's distress, I could never get comfortable. She knew something was not right. We arrived late at night and I had to leave Gail to struggle with our suitcases across the long, deserted station to the exit on the other side of the track.

Our new base, the Hotel Il Pellicano, was as welcoming as the first, but by now it was becoming clear that although I was eating more than I had done recently, my weight was falling. Gail noticed that I had begun to look thinner again.

I started to experience violent pains towards the end of a meal, and found I was vomiting up more food than I was able to eat. Meals became an endurance test yet again.

When we came home a week later I still felt that, for all its flaws, the holiday had been an extraordinary success. But as soon as I got back to London Gail insisted that I phone the Marsden and tell them of my difficulties. Come in as soon as possible, they told me. And so the process began again.

This time, somehow or other, we were able to transcend the difficulties that would have seemed almost insuperable many years ago. I had a series of tests at the Marsden immediately but the first results seemed all right. I was relieved, if not relaxed.

A few days later I visited my publisher, Tim Whiting, at Little, Brown's offices on Victoria Embankment. I was there to discuss with Tim and my editor Zoe Gullen the final draft of the updated *Unfinished Revolution*. This task, which had caused me so much heartache, was over at last.

The phone rang. It was the Marsden for me. Tim steered me into a small quiet room and left me to take it.

My blood tumour marker had increased from 5 per cent to 58 per cent.

I knew then the game was up.

I called Gail and she agreed. She more than agreed. She knew too.

She told me she had been under the impression that my desperation in finishing the politics book and writing the early chapters of this one was born of a desire to get everything down before I died. I had to admit that I too had a lingering feeling that the moment I finished the second book, my purpose in life would be completed and the end would begin.

The Marsden sent me for an immediate scan and the tone of their instruction clearly indicated that something menacing had emerged. At that moment, I made a decision: I would rather face this with acceptance. What was happening was that the cancer had come back.

I went in at about five in the evening and was told that whatever happened I would have to stay in that night so they could sort this out. I knew then that we had reached a critical moment.

Gail arrived looking flustered but strong. We sat ourselves in the day unit at about half-past eight. The neon light was glaring. The industrial cleaners were starting their nightly work. This was a kind place, but we felt beleaguered and isolated.

Through the glass doors we could see David Cunningham

and his team, looking scared and clearly acutely worried about me. Eventually, Kaz Mochlinski emerged to tell me that the cancer had indeed returned, this time in the lymph nodes above and below the radiotherapy area.

David came in and was very clear, serious and stark. I asked him what my worst-case prognosis was.

'Three months,' he said.

Gail asked what the best case was.

'Three months.'

I described earlier what it is like to be told for the first time that you have cancer. You instinctively believe you can defeat it. Being informed of a first recurrence was confusing. It should not have happened and made no sense to me. Only through that long conversation with Tony Blair did I feel able to make sense of it by understanding that cancer wanted more from me, and that I had to change more and to develop a stronger sense of purpose.

But the third diagnosis of cancer was entirely different.

This was like being hit by a ten-ton truck on a wet, cold night in Indiana.

The reality, the possibility, the certainty of death suddenly became absolutely real. Completely inevitable and frankly frightening. In a moment we had moved from a sense of having some control to feeling complete loss of influence. We were at the mercy of events now.

I had just a very few months to live.

*

David was magnificent. He told us that the cancer could be treated and listed our options, but there was no doubting how contingent it all was.

I would not last more than three months. We were no longer acting in a normal patient–doctor relationship, in which cure or recovery is the aim, but as a team planning how to manage my death.

Gail and I left that meeting feeling more mauled by events than at any of the other cancer meetings. Emotionally this seemed almost unrecoverable.

We arranged the next few days' logistics. I would move into the Marsden almost immediately and have a new feeding tube put in, and the next day would start the chemotherapy that in theory would continue for six months.

Everything was now happening very fast. The speed of this plan of action was impressive, but it also gave me a rather alarming sense of the vulnerability and impotency of my position.

Other people tried to buoy up my spirits. Mike Griffin called from Newcastle to say that the cancer was still treatable, even if only in the context of a disease that was now out of our control.

I phoned Tony Blair and for the first time in our long professional and personal relationship he did not quite know what to say. But he recovered soon enough.

We got through the weekend and planned what was supposed to be a one-night stop in the Marsden. And once again we encountered the familiar contours of the cancer sufferer's life.

Once again, we turned up early and nervous. Once again, there was the same old business of finding a room. Once again we had to begin establishing relationships with staff at the hospital, building a micro-community.

I had been told quite explicitly that with an operation like this there was a degree of risk of leakage and other side effects. But the operation was conducted with great professionalism by Satvinder Mudan, the surgeon who had entered my life at the very beginning of my cancer journey and who now had a part to play as it neared its end.

He was as confident and opinionated and charming as I remembered him. The operation was scheduled for the Monday and he delayed a flight to China in order to perform it himself.

Because of the nature of the two previous oesophageal operations I had undergone, it was a difficult procedure, but we were hopeful. As it turned out, the operation went well, but there was cancer evident in the lymph nodes, on the bowels and elsewhere.

That night the pain began.

It came excruciatingly and intensely through my digestive system. Not only did it hurt a great deal, it also indicated that there might be a leak. If there was, that would delay chemotherapy. If chemotherapy was delayed, my death might not be.

It was imperative to start chemotherapy as quickly as possible. David Cunningham, whom I had found generally to be a cautious man, was determined to begin it the following day. That was both efficient and chilling. The cancer had to be killed fast, otherwise it would kill me.

That was his position at the beginning of the morning. By the next day all had changed yet again.

The pain seemed to arise from a leakage or a build-up of fluids that might quickly go away. But this still meant the chemo was going to be delayed, and delayed chemo would inevitably hasten my death.

The next night was worse. I was suffused with discomfort and generally in pain. And I was taking my first feeds via the new tube. This produced a bitterness in my mouth and a feeling of sickness that was nearly intolerable. I was vomiting often. And I began to suffer delusions because of all the drugs I was taking.

This continued day after day until it was decided that the only thing to do was to stop all forms of treatment and all food and see what happened. It worked. My gut calmed down and by Friday I felt that the worst was over.

But I believed, and so did Gail, that there was now a good chance I would not leave the hospital again.

By mid-afternoon on the Tuesday after the operation, David came for a meeting. He told us he was changing his strategy and pushing back the chemotherapy for at least a week, possibly two. It was clear that things were veering off course.

He told us that we were all in this together, but I could sense from his grave tone his foreboding about the risks. He was having to navigate a slow ship across a rough sea, in visibility too poor for us to see where we were headed.

Saturday morning. Gail came to visit me in hospital and thus began three of the most extraordinary days of my life. I have never been a particularly emotional person but now I could see no alternative but to show her how I felt about everything that had happened and everything to come. I looked at Gail and wept.

I wept for the lost opportunities. I wept for the lost moments of happiness. And in the end, I wept for the lost companionship. I had never before been able to talk to her, or anyone else, with such intensity.

The power of cancer was proving much greater than the power of death. Until now I had always seen life as a succession of doors with names on them. Names like Birth, First Job, Marriage, Children, Retirement. And at almost every threshold I had crossed there was some genuine conceptual connection between what I expected to happen and what actually did. I felt this was dramatically not true of the door marked Death. When it comes to death there is a great gap between the name on the door and the reality.

I know that everyone has a different view of death, a

different perspective on it, but I think they also share a consensus that death is wrong and belongs to another time and place.

Death is usually depicted as a time of decline, of growing irrelevance, as the ending of growth, the cessation of contribution. To some extent those things may be true. But for the dying themselves, like me, there is another dynamic at work: the sheer intensity of death leads us to assess our world in ways we have never done before, each contributing to a kind of pre-death moment of judgment.

For some it is God who judges us. That may be so, but I suspect that in fact it is we who judge ourselves. The unvarnished certainty that you are going to die within a certain period of time is an immensely powerful thing. It provides the opportunity for fulfilment and the experience of extraordinary depths of feeling and the chance of reconciliation that would never otherwise occur.

I spoke to David Sturgeon, a respected consultant psychiatrist, about these views. He said two things to me that affected me deeply.

The first was that the only way to have a good death is to accept it. The second was to understand that for many people, if not most, death is the most important time of life.

I remember very clearly seeing my daughters born and my father die. Both experiences had equal power. The babies arrived largely shorn of consciousness; my father, aged seventy-eight, departed with years of experience of life. What you are at the beginning of the journey is as important as what you are at the end.

Death is not frightening if you accept it. It is a time for immense change and transformation, a time to fulfil yourself and others, and a chance in a small way to change the world.

And these three days with Gail were life-changing for me. I was prepared to smash down my emotional barricades and be fully open and honest with her. I was ready to show her my acceptance of death and my vulnerability.

She responded in the same way, and by the afternoon our relationship had reached an intensity that we had never touched before.

The following day, Sunday, was different. Gail came to my room in a more angry frame of mind. At first she was cross with me over some small incident with Grace, but then she transferred most of her anger to an episode from many years earlier in our marriage. I had wanted us to move home to be nearer to good state schools for our daughters. She had wanted to stay in a house she loved. I had prevailed.

This was what she was angry about. She was saying: why did you do this? Why did you move me and my family from a lovely house to one we didn't like so much, in another part of London?

Times like this, when I had taken such an abrupt and brutal approach, or when I had spent night after night conducting focus groups, neglecting the kids, who were asking for my help and not always getting it, troubled her. And she said so.

She also felt that I had indulged in a long-term strategy of destruction in which, after she had built up wonderful houses or institutions, I would almost always destroy them. I half-expected her to ask: what have you been on all these years? But she did not.

I could see for the first time that some of my actions had been driven less by a need for power in our relationship than by my own insecurity about it. Now I could see how wrong I was, both about Gail and myself.

On the other hand, I could see that I had hugely under-estimated her fantastic, almost unlimited skills. It had taken living on Planet Cancer, and in particular realising I was close to death, for me to see these for what they were.

My response to Gail's anger was to accept it, to apologise and to show that I understood that what I had done was wrong. I replied: 'Well, you are right to be angry, quite honestly.' And then, after that, we moved on to a different place, one we have never left.

I realised that there was a huge process of reckoning to be done.

Reckoning is not some concept that just happens by itself. It is not going to happen after you die. You have to look into your life. And you think, oh my God, these are the things I have done. I have a little bit of time here; I can resolve them.

I have done a lot of that with Gail, and I have done the same with others, including the children. But of course I have known Gail for forty years – we have had a lot of time together, and we still have a little time. It is different for my children. They are young, twenty-five and twenty-two, and are trying to come to terms with all of this. Sorting things out, individually or between us, is more rushed and difficult in some ways. But the honest truth is that I have found that if one has the will and the intention, it is possible to effect enormous transformation.

I have always got on moderately well with my sister, Jill, but never super well. Now, because of this situation and because of the conversations that we have had as a result of it, we are getting on much better than ever. There has been time to make these changes.

These reckonings with people whom I love would not have happened were it not for our knowledge and acceptance that I will die of cancer soon. Because they know I am going to die and I know that I am going to die, we are willing to do it. But because I have been given this little bit of time, we are also *able* to do it. In this way death gives meaning to life.

On Monday, the final day of my stint at the Marsden, the tenor of our conversation changed again. Now we looked to the future. We began talking about buying a new flat for

Gail and the best way forward for her without me. We discussed the best ways for her to develop her life.

We had moved in three days from nostalgia, via anger about the past, to a sweet and meaningful discussion of the future. I believe this was a transcendent moment in our marriage, after which we moved to a new level of understanding of each other.

Gail has changed, I think permanently. This has not been just a surface change either. It is a change that is deeper and better rooted than that. She has become slowly and surely a different person. Warmer, less private, more open. She has begun to trust me more. Her response to my cancer in its terminal stages has been unbelievably tender and loving. This love is of a degree and intensity I have almost never felt before.

There have been good times and bad times. But these are new times.

The Death Zone

I am going to die. My death is inevitable and is likely to come within the next few weeks, perhaps even within the next few days. It is real. It is a fact of my life. There is no opportunity to cop out or dissemble. There is no way to avoid it. It is there. I am going to die soon. As long as I keep telling myself that and do not seek to evade it, I am in the right place.

The awareness of death that I had throughout my life was, I see now, an illusion. Even when the doctors said there was a 25 per cent chance I would die, then a 60 per cent chance, there was always an escape. It is only when they said: Philip Gould, *you* are going to die. Get used to it. This is going to happen in months or weeks but it *is* going to happen. Only then do you become aware of death, and suddenly life screams at you with its intensity.

The doctors who matter, the doctors you trust, always confront this reality. They tell you: sooner rather than later, you are going to die. For example, at the beginning of this process I went on television and said, 'Well, they told me I've probably got three months to live.' I went along, saw my doctor and said, 'Yeah, three months to live,' and he said, 'No, that was six weeks ago. You have just six weeks left now.' And that absolute harshness and clarity and real connection to the time you possibly have to live is the key to this.

I believe that only when you accept death can you free yourself from it, deal with it, move forward from it. Acceptance is the key.

Every single time you try to tell yourself 'Yeah, but . . .' or 'OK, it's tough, but . . .' or 'OK, it's difficult, but maybe . . .' that is a lie. And that lie will stop you living properly, and it will stop you having a good death.

Whenever I start to deviate from acceptance and start to think, 'Yeah, OK, maybe . . .' or if I hear someone saying it, even someone I love, I say: 'Look, your dad is going to die, your husband is going to die . . . There is no alternative to this, it is going to happen.'

At that moment you gain freedom. You gain power. You gain courage.

That is what I think about the nature of death. I know that people deal with death in different ways. If people wish to use denial, then fair enough. That is their decision. However, denial is not for me at all.

And I am absolutely sure from my understanding of life, my understanding of death, my understanding of all there is to do with these complex issues, that you have to be honest and you have to be true to yourself and you have to accept.

When you reach that place where you have been told – and you believe – that you are going to die within a certain amount of time: that is the Death Zone.

If you know you are dying but say: 'Well, I'm not in the Death Zone because it is not yet certain' – in other words, that it is not certain you are going to die yet, that it might be in a year, or two – then you are in denial.

This is just a way of saying: 'Actually, I'm in the Death Zone ... but I'm not in the Death Zone.' That will not work. You have to accept the fact, accept that you are going to die.

If you accept that, then progress is possible. And not just progress, which we will talk about later, but all manner of things are possible. But you have to accept that you are about to die.

I absolutely feel that the moment I accepted death and looked it in the eye and faced it, then I had – not defeated death, you cannot defeat death – freed myself from death. I think I have shown myself that I have the courage to be able to transcend death. Maybe I cannot beat death, but death cannot beat me.

The key is to look death squarely in the eye without blinking. I know that sounds arrogant, but I believe it to be true.

My wife and I went to see a vicar about my funeral arrangements. We were so nervous we were all over the place. We did not know what we were doing. But as the hour passed, calmness came, and we realised we were not frightened of death any more. We were facing death by looking it in the eye, and that gave us freedom.

Earlier this week, I had a couple of really tough nights. My breathing was bad, my digestive system was bad, my diarrhoea was bad, my coughing was bad. Everything was bad. Gail was in a bad state too.

I just lay there and thought: 'OK, this *is* bad. But this is death, and as long as I look death in the eye and as long as I accept it, I can choose – to an extent at least – the kind of death that I want. I have some freedom, I have some power here. I have the possibility to shape for myself my own death.'

At that moment I had a sense of freedom, and every time I experience that I am free of death, for a moment at least.

Fear of death is crucial to our understanding, but this idea of facing it square on is a core one for me, probably *the* core one, and it is the one that works best for me.

Entering the Death Zone provided a process through which, step by step, I became able to cope with the reality of dying.

I had always expected, ever since my first diagnosis of

cancer four or so years ago, that I would be able to cope with it to some extent. Then, when I had my first chemotherapy, I was terrified. In a way, chemotherapy is a symbolic, iconic representation of cancer. It comes with these tubes, these side effects, these horrible things that seem so awful to contemplate as happening to you.

Before it started I thought: I simply cannot do this. I cannot do chemotherapy. It is too painful. It is too horrible.

But you do it.

Then the people treating you say: 'By the way, mate, you are not going to have an oesophagus, you're not going to have any of this or that or here or there, and you will never eat normally ever again.'

And you get used to that.

Then you realise – whatever they throw at you, you can deal with it.

And that is because your body and your mind have an extraordinary capacity to deal with what is going to come later. It is just an amazing thing. You learn how to cope with these challenges, one after another. There is more in the human body than you will ever understand, more physically, more emotionally, more spiritually, more religiously, even. The body can cope. You can cope. You can do it. You can deal with the pain, you can deal with the discomfort, you can deal with the uncertainty, you can deal with it all. It is possible to deal with it all.

Realising that changes you as a person.

*

Then there is the matter of courage.

You think: God, I'm scared, I'm a coward.

I thought I was a coward. I was the kind of guy who was frightened to go too fast on a bike in the evening. Too frightened to go on the big rides at Alton Towers, or do any of the scary swimming stuff, or even to duck my head under water. I just did not have the courage to do these things.

But when cancer came, bringing with it a great deal of fear and pain, I found I could deal with it. Time and time again I found the courage to deal with this acute and terrible pain.

The pain was and is bad. It is slow and mundane, day after day after day of pain, feeling sick, vomiting. Endless, endless, endless pain. But you get to be able to endure it. However horrible it is, cancer prepares you for what comes next. It prepared me. It braced me too for the fact that it might return; and when it did return, it prepared me to understand that it might come back in a much worse form.

It prepared me for all that, and then it tested me again. It said, actually, this is going to come back, and frankly it may come back in part because of human error. I am not, by the way, saying that necessarily happened. But nonetheless human error was a factor.

You have to live with that huge thing too. You live with the possibility that human error caused this.

So you are dealing all the time with a vast number of things. Fear. Uncertainty. Pain. And what I have found is that, as it goes on, you get stronger and stronger and stronger and freer and freer and freer. All the way through my cancer journey, my body and my mind have been able to cope with the next stage. Cancer prepares you to take the next step, even as you are completing the one before. In the end you lose your fear of the next step because you know you will be able to take it.

We all have to endure pain, but it gets in the way. Some believe that through pain you gain enlightenment. My experience has been quite prosaic. If I feel pain I stop. My creativity falls away. I really do not like pain.

I would be one week on chemo and one week off, and the week when I was not undergoing chemo was the creative week for me. In the non-chemo week I was able to write and do things.

The more pain can be got rid of, the better. What you need in the Death Zone are as many good quality days as you can possibly have, with your friends and with your relatives and with your books, or whatever it is you want. Get rid of pain as best you can. I really do not care how you do it.

I try to get rid of pain straight away myself. It does not help me in my creativity, it does not help me with my self-expression, it does not help me build relationships. Even when the kids talk to me they cannot have a proper conversation if I am in pain.

What's the point of pain if it does not do me any good?

The only thing I ever really gained from pain came when I was suffering the most acute form of it in my entire life. I had just undergone the surgery in Newcastle. It hurt so badly that I remember thinking: God, I understand now what it is like to have pain.

And I found myself wanting to say to the world, I feel your pain and understand the pain you are feeling. I wanted to send an empathetic message to everyone.

When I had my second recurrence, the medical staff said: 'Look, let's be honest, you've got seven lymph nodes full of cancer, it's not good.'

When I asked the doctor what my chances were, he looked down and shuffled his papers a bit, and I knew then that the game was probably up. I did not know what to do. I had no sense of purpose. I was lost.

But I found a purpose. To begin with, it was just to find what it was in this new stage of life that would give me meaning. In other words, finding a purpose became my purpose.

Then came that terrible Friday morning when the hospital rang to say: 'Now you've gone through the 5 per cent tumour marker up to the 58 per cent marker.'

It was all over – completely and clearly.

I was not going to make it unless I was very lucky. No, I was not going to make it. That is what I mean by being honest. Fuck it. You must be honest.

*

Gail and I went to one absolutely bleak late-night session where the hospital staff were checking the scans. They were wonderful people but what they had to say was in effect: 'Look, you've got cancer all over the place, and you know it is going to kill you. It is going to kill you in three months, four months or five months, but it *is* going to kill you.' There was no question about it at all and I knew that. It was kind of like being hit by a roller-coaster, it was so hard.

Georgia, quoting Leonard Cohen, always says there is a crack in everything, that's how the light gets in. There was no crack here. This was pure darkness and death. Whenever I tried to move the conversation on, the doctor kept saying: 'You are going to die and that is that.'

Gail and I just looked at each other and started to cry. I cried endlessly for hours, I was so sad. We knew this was it and we knew there was no escape, and so we cried.

A day later we bounced back. We moved to a different place and a different time. It was a totally transcendent moment. I saw now that the purpose I had been seeking was to give as much love as I could. Even though I was dying I knew that was what I had to do. It was clear, there was absolutely no ambivalence about it. I was dying, I had to make the most of that and my purpose was explicit. And so my death became my life.

And my life gained a kind of intensity that it had never had before. It gained a quality and a power that it had never had before.

I have my wife and my children here for me at this moment, because I am defining myself now through death, I'm giving meaning to myself through death. Without that I do not know what I would do. I need family and I need meaning and they converge into the same thing in the end. I do not see how I could get through this without the support of my family. It would be absolutely impossible to do that. I cannot envisage how anyone could do that.

I rely upon my family enormously, almost completely. I try to lead them. I try to inspire them. I try to show strength. It is me who is dying but me who has to show them a way forward.

I do not suppose there are many people in the world who know they have fewer than three months to live, who are trying to articulate what it feels like as I am doing now. I do not mean to suggest that only I am articulate enough to say these things, but that this is a unique opportunity for me.

I want to write and talk about dying. It is important for me to do that. It is an extraordinary experience to know you just have these few months, or weeks, or days and to be able to articulate your feelings about that.

I want to say something else as well, because this is not a seminar. In six weeks or less, I will be dead. Before then, I will face huge fear. This is the real, unavoidable experience that is coming unstoppably my way.

The moment you accept the imminence of death, fear disappears – up to a point. The other night, my blood levels had fallen, which is bad. And in general, my tests were not as good as I would have liked, and I felt fear. I felt the future rushing towards me. Time was running out. Maybe soon I would be in a hospice, and once I went there I might not escape.

I could feel it happening and it is inevitable that you feel fear. You can conquer it, but you cannot, in all honesty, obliterate it, and it is wrong even to suggest that you can. Fear is still there.

Now what I say every time is, go to the fear, seek it out. Be like a fear-seeking missile. It works, not always but most of the time. Certainly, looking at fear this way is essential. The moment you move towards fear, the closer you move towards the avoidance of fear, the conquering of fear, and the better it is.

This strategy is paradoxical of course. Obviously it is better to have less fear rather than more, but we are in one big paradox here. It is death that gives intensity to life. All of us know this, all of us living in the Death Zone. I talk to people like myself about this all the time: only through death and the fear of death do you feel this intensity.

That is the key to it. Intensity comes from knowing you will die and knowing you are dying. This is particularly true when you are given the death sentence, as I was. Suddenly you can go for a walk in the park and have a moment of ecstasy. I go to the Frieze Art Fair in Regent's Park opposite our house. I go to the exhibition tent and I sit there and have a coffee and I feel ecstasy after ecstasy after ecstasy. This is built upon this feeling of certainty, of knowledge, of death. There is ecstasy because I am not dead yet.

I mentioned earlier that I had a terrible night recently. It could not really have been much rougher; I was very, very tired and was sick for most of the night. I had to make maybe a dozen trips to the loo and was feeling generally just dreadful. Gail stayed with me as I struggled.

In the morning she came in to see me and by this time I did not look good. Gail just gave me this smile of tenderness that was almost beyond words it was so wonderful. The tenderness she showed me was beyond anything I could ever have expected. It was extraordinary. I felt security. I felt, finally, I am safe at home.

I knew then that the tenderness I saw on her face was utterly dependent upon the knowledge that I was going to die, and that I would soon be dead. Without that knowledge of death there would have been no such tenderness, but with it, such tenderness was possible. Death is immensely cruel but also immensely powerful.

I am enjoying my death. There is no question I am having the most fulfilling time of my life. I am having in many ways the most enjoyable time of my life. I am having these moments of ecstasy. I am having the closest relationships with all of my family. This is the most intense time of my life.

Why should all enjoyment stop the moment someone tells you that you are going to die? Of course it does not stop. Death has many components. You do feel sadness. I am leaving my children and my wife. Georgia has said to me: 'Dad, I want you to be there when I get married, when I first have a child.' Grace has said similar things.

What I want to say to my daughters is that this is the most exciting and extraordinary journey of my life. My only regret is that it will end, and end soon. I would like to be on this journey with you for ever and a day. I want to be with you all the time. I know that it is not possible, but I wish profoundly that it was. Your own journeys lie ahead of you and you will take what I have started and turn it into something much more magnificent, much more extraordinary.

Death can leave you feeling incomplete and it is sad. But it is also the process of transformation and change and excitement. It is beyond my moral or philosophical understanding to say which sides of this experience are most important. I just do not know.

But I do know this. I have had more moments of happiness in the last five months than in the last five years. I have had more moments of private ecstasy than for a very long time. I feel at peace with the world.

So there are moments of intense enjoyment. The great balance in the Death Zone rests between the pain and the gain. Without doubt, for me the gain has been greater than the pain.

The opportunity, the possibility, the chance of fulfilment makes this the most extraordinary and important time of your life. Can you enjoy it? Yes, you can. Should you enjoy it? Well, if you can, yes!

I feel well equipped for this last stage largely because of the help I have been given. Death sounds so frightening, but so did cancer. So did chemotherapy. So did surgery. All these things are frightening and all of these things are tough.

But at the end we have it within ourselves to cope with them.

I was absolutely sure when I was diagnosed with cancer that I wanted – I took an instinctive decision – to share this experience with the world, and I thought I had to do it. I was absolutely determined to communicate in some way to the world what had happened, and I wanted to do it and I did it.

There is a misconception in the way that death is projected and communicated. I would not say that black becomes white or white becomes black but there is definitely a misconception.

Changing that is my purpose now. I am attempting to transform perceptions of death rather as I tried to transform perceptions of politics. I want to lead people to understand that what they are told about death is not necessarily the reality.

Life is a dialectical process. It is not linear. One moves forward dialectically. You follow a path, learn from that, and you change. You take another path. Learn from that. And so on.

I worked in advertising, which I loved. I then did politics, which I absolutely loved. After many more changes I entered the world of cancer, which is a very powerful world and one that I hope I have helped people understand better with my writing about it. Now I have entered the world of death: the Death Zone. And my impression is that people want to know about that too.

Now, am I going too far? Have I crossed barriers? I think that probably I might have done. I have not been as sensitive as I should to the needs of Gail, Georgia and Grace, let alone those of my wider family. I was determined to press ahead, to do this.

I think it is fair to say I have not been anywhere near attentive enough to the people I love during this period. I was determined to use this sense of purpose to drive us forward, but it is a legitimate complaint that certain lines in the sand have been crossed. I decided that I would cross those lines. I decided that I would go further than might be wise, and I know that other people might disagree with what I did.

Gail has carefully read everything I have written on the subject. Grace has read it, and Georgia has read it too. But I am making the decisions here, nobody else, and there is, I recognise, an arrogance involved and a lack of humility.

So many people told me to tell the truth. So many doctors, so many surgeons, so many people kept on coming back and saying, 'Please tell the truth.' Especially about the surgery I underwent. So I think I have done the right thing. I have been careful – though perhaps not careful enough. But I would do it again, for sure.

I think the gains have been enormous. The gains for Gail have certainly been enormous. She has changed from someone who was private about cancer and about death to someone who wants to be public about it and who now actually wants more information to be put out there.

The kids are starting to get anxious, even a bit angry about things sometimes. Death is about abandonment. Everybody will have concerns and feel sadness and anger about abandonment. I can see that. But nonetheless the children too believe there have been gains as well as losses. What I have done in talking and writing about my illness has been hugely important for us, and not the kind of thing I could do too often. I have been nervous about it all the way through. But I was determined to do it and I am determined to continue doing it as long as I can.

The point of life is that you evolve, change, develop, and become a different person. The idea is that life is something that you actually *do*.

I certainly do not think that a sudden, unexpected death – dropping dead, as they say – would be better than what confronts me. You would lose so much. Of course, it would be nice to avoid confronting death, nice to blunt that sharp edge. And you would avoid a lot of pain, I suppose. But I think those things are far outweighed by the things you gain from knowing that you are going to die and having the chance to act on that knowledge.

To have three months, or two months, or one month, or even a week in which to actually sit down and to fulfil and complete your relationships is almost the greatest gift that death can offer. If you can accept death, the process of grieving that follows may still be intense but it will pass and will ultimately be fulfilling and elevating. And if you can look death in the eye and accept it, and then fulfil your relationships, that is healing.

In the last few weeks I have had to come to terms with all that I have done in sixty years of living. Making sense of this is important. And it is not a passive process of reconciliation but an active one.

All this experience comes together. All the extraordinary connections and relationships made during a relatively long life must be considered. And in the many reconciliations and reckonings of this process there is the power of fulfilment. This is when you surge forward and grow. I feel I am surging forward and growing at a pace that I have never experienced before.

This surge of understanding takes you into a different state of being. All of us tend to think in terms of linear time. One thing follows another. But this is only one form of time's many complexities. I can no longer think like that.

What good is it to me to think in terms of conventional time? Six months or nine months no longer exist for me. So I am trying to make sense of the world not through time but through emotion, through relationships, through feeling.

I am looking at the world through this great collection of emotions and relationships and progressions and changes. All at once. That is what is happening for me now. When I try to push forward in terms of conventional time, to look ahead, to count the minutes or the hours or the days, sooner rather than later I hit a solid rock: I am dead on the other side of this.

I think instead in terms of other, richer conceptions of progression – relationships, emotional connection, spiritual understanding, the sense of God, the sense of divinity. There is no future for me now so I am flowing back and this here, now, is the place for everything. Here, now, is where I live, where all these ideas and feelings circle on themselves.

Of course, for a short while at least, I can look forward to tomorrow. I have looked forward to every single day this week and every single day this week has been better than the day that preceded it. Every single moment is almost better than the moment that preceded it.

I feel nothing but optimism. I know that the future will be bad. I know that it will be difficult. I know that there will be those horrible moments when the stomach does this and the stomach does that, and God knows what else. I know all that.

But life cannot be better than this. I cannot feel better than this. I do not see how life can be better for me than this. I know how life can be better for those who care for me and love me. I understand that, I do not try to deny that. But for me, even though this may well be the worst of times, it is also the best of times.

Given all that I have said here I think it is reasonable to ask what I would do if I was offered the chance to have the death sentence suddenly, miraculously, lifted. Would I prefer that, even if I had to give up all the things that I have found here in the Death Zone? It is a difficult question.

I would have to accept the offer for the sake of Gail and for the kids. I do understand that my family wants more time with me and I respect that. But I believe that this is the right place for me and I want to be here in this state of mind and to die in it if I can. I am, I hope anyway, a different and better person than the one I was before this happened.

This is what I am meant to be. This is what I am meant

to do. I have to make this more than just a good intention. By my example, I want to change things for other people as well.

I am comfortable with my life now. This is a frightening process, of course. But it is also true that it is possible to confront that fear and transcend it. You go to another place. You really do.

I have had a lot worse happen to me in the last four years than is going to happen in the next four weeks. It will be difficult but I hope, I believe, I think, ultimately it will be sublime. That is not to say it will be sublime in some great religious sense, although it might be, but I believe there will be a quality of the sublime about it.

I feel very calm. I feel at rest. I have found that the experience of the last few weeks has been as good as it is possible for the experience to be. And that has been typical of my life since I entered the Death Zone.

Going to my Grave

When I was recovering from my surgery in Newcastle I began to think once again about arranging my own burial plot. So I called Highgate Cemetery and asked if they had any plots. They did, I was told, and I was given the name of a man to speak to about it. And then, what with one thing and another, I forgot about the idea.

When I was diagnosed as being terminally ill, and told that my death was coming sooner rather than later, I remembered again. I called the number I had been given. The person I had been told to contact had left the cemetery but the man on the end of the phone said he would look after me anyway.

'I'll do it,' he said. 'My name is Victor. I'm the grave-digger.'

Of course I expected Victor to be a six-foot-six giant with a big shovel over one shoulder. And when I met him he turned out to be a six-foot-six giant with a shovel over one shoulder.

Victor Herman deals all the time with people who are dying, and quite often with people like me who are about to die. He is the sexton, and although he has worked at Highgate for twenty-two years, he actually dug his first grave there ten years before that, when he was fourteen. His father had been the head gravedigger there for years and so he and his family were part of the history of the whole place.

Victor and I and Gail wandered around the cemetery a couple of times. He would suggest a spot here or there, but they were not the kind of places I wanted.

I wanted a bigger plot, somewhere that could become almost a communal place for our family and friends. I was looking not so much for a burial plot as a burial place, I suppose, a meeting place, something physical that you could see and connect to.

Victor may be big but he is gentle with it: he was wonderful with Gail. He gave her great comfort because he has had so much experience of dealing with death.

He dealt with us beautifully. It was a wonderful morning and at last we chose a spot.

Finding a physical place for me was a huge step forward. On the one hand it was a place to which people who are still alive can come and connect to me. For my daughters in particular that would be a good thing. And on the other hand it enabled me to see the place where I was going to spend eternity. Here was the place where my family and friends could come to find me.

And perhaps not only people who knew me. There will be people about the place looking at the graves, looking at my grave, so it will be almost a communal meeting point between the dead and the living. It sounds very romantic, I know. But the dead and the living are both part of our lives. It gives me great comfort to know that I will be there.

This morning I stood at my grave and I thought: God, I do feel very, very happy to be going to this place. That is a small victory for a different view of death.

As this process goes on, as death gets closer, my experiences become more and more tense, but also more and more joyful. They are surprising, too. Things happen that I would not have expected to happen. Coincidences occur. I find I have entered a world which is not as I thought it would be. It is much better than I thought it would be. The ground rules, the nature of reality, in this world are different.

I knew it would be special this morning when we went to my grave, and it was. I was photographed at my place of interment. I am now alive but later I will be dead. It was very powerful and led to a whole series of connections that were quite surprising and unexpected.

This morning, I did not feel that I was in a dead place.

I did not think this morning that I was in a place from which energy had gone, at which the process of decline was starting. I did not feel that this was somehow the beginning of decay.

Instead I saw that this too was life. It was the taking of us from what we are to being something different. And that, I think, is the process of death.

I had an absolutely wonderful trip yesterday with my two daughters. It did not start that way. I was not feeling well and I was in and out of the car before we began. So we all felt a bit frazzled and tense as we set off. But as we travelled away from London, things changed.

We went to all the places where I used to spend my time as a young boy. We went from one meaningful place to another. We went to my school, to my childhood home, to the place where I used to play football, where I used to play sport.

We had a house on a canal and I remember this canal as always being quite pretty. It was so pretty yesterday when we visited.

We went to my parents' graves and I told Georgia and Grace, not for the first time, that there is still not a day that goes past that I do not miss them.

Every place we went imparted a certain power to our journey, and so as we went from one to another the feelings became more and more powerful, until by the end we were all in a state of joy. We were suddenly happy as a family and at the end Georgia said: 'It was the most perfect day.'

And this on the back of a couple of days which had been among the most difficult I have had recently. There was a quality of specialness about that day that would not have been possible were it not that the stakes were so high. It would not have happened were it not for us knowing and accepting that I would die of cancer soon.

My daughters know I am going to die and I know that I am going to die. In those circumstances we are all willing to do something as potentially difficult and upsetting as making this journey together back into my past.

Death gives meaning to life and the knowledge that you are going to die one day gives you the sense that there is meaning in your life. When you are going to die soon, you really do feel the absolute intensity of life. Life becomes completely precious, not just because there is so little of it left but because the actual nature of experience is more fulfilling, more protean than it was before. I feel there are somehow more molecules moving around the room now.

Death is going to happen to everybody, but it is happening to me now.

A few more days passed. We were outside London, enjoying the countryside and bringing the family together as I prepared for the next round of chemotherapy. Over the weekend I noticed I was experiencing a form of breath-lessness. I could not walk up the stairs or move quickly or dramatically without having difficulty breathing.

We waited until Tuesday before doing anything about it because that was the day I was due in hospital to start that next round of treatment. The medical staff took one look at me and steered me away from chemotherapy and towards a new diagnosis. I had blood tests and X-rays.

The results were clear. A dangerous level of infection had entered my lungs and there was also widespread inflammation, which was the cause of my breathlessness. It was clear that my body would be unable to cope with the ravages of treatment.

On Thursday 3 November, David Cunningham comes in to see me entirely alone. He leaves his entourage outside. He tells me that it does not look as though the therapies and, in particular, the steroids they have been giving me are having the desired effect. Some of my blood tracings are good, others are not.

I ask him what the worst case is for me now.

Three to five days, he says.

What is the best case?

Three or four weeks.

Just as being told I had three months to live had been a much bigger shock than any bad news I had received before, this new timetable, being told I might die in three days, is another quantum leap.

On hearing previous diagnoses I was uncertain about the future. This time I am not. I know my purpose.

I am endeavouring to be honest about the reality of death. I am trying to make clear its importance and help inspire others as they move towards it.

I know how hard this is to do but I want to try.

In her book *On Death and Dying*, Elisabeth Kübler-Ross says that with love this period can be the most fulfilling and extraordinary time of life. I am sure she is right. Death provides the creative tension in everybody's life, but when you enter the Death Zone the intensity is either overwhelming or extraordinary in its possibilities.

I have no doubt that this pre-death period is the most important and potentially the most fulfilling and the most inspirational time of my life. In this world, conventional time becomes meaningless. You map your course according to the coordinates of emotion and feelings, compassion and love.

I am approaching the door marked Death. What lies beyond it may be the worst of things. But I believe it will be the best of things.

Four Days Left to Change the World

Georgia Gould

Dad went into the Marsden for the last time on the Tuesday. He was not rushed in; it was his routine chemotherapy appointment.

We had been preparing for a long period of steady decline, of hospices, of slowing down and goodbyes. We had lived with cancer for so long that we were used to his periods of gauntness and sickness, used to seeing his body wasted and thin, his skin dry and peeling. These things were not necessarily signs of impending death but reactions to the treatment – the scars of cancer.

We knew, of course, his prognosis. His cancer was terminal. We were two months into the three that Professor

Cunningham had predicted for him. Death had become something we lived with: making group tours of Highgate Cemetery, poring over funeral plans and strategising for posthumous publication. But, at least to me, death still always felt one step removed. Dad was always there, an active, engaged participant in the discussion – very much alive.

Even Dad, who relentlessly faced up to the truth of his condition, had moments when reality escaped him. I remember him saying that he had been sitting admiring his new shoes, thinking they looked smart enough for the funeral – before catching himself and remembering he would not actually be attending the funeral, at least not in a way that he need worry about shoes. He would joke that he had made such a fuss of dying that he needed a contingency plan if he did not die when he had predicted.

When someone is so full of life, humour, wisdom, so much themselves, it is easy not to see their body wasting away, easy to forget how stark the difference is between life and death. There is a big space between knowledge and acceptance.

Dad was determinedly trying to prepare my sister and me for his death. He knew better than us how highly we all had to value the time left. He invested everything he could in giving us the tools we would need for life, answering questions we did not even know we would have for him.

*

On the Thursday before he went into hospital he had organised a trip to Brookwood, the place where he grew up. This still stands out for me as a perfect day.

I had been up all night finishing a report. My sister, Grace, was stressed about her work. But Dad was insistent there would not be another chance for us to go together. And so we went. Dad had organised a car as Mum was not around and she is still the only member of the family who can drive. Dad was struggling with nausea and we had to stop and go back twice for more anti-sickness medication. But he took all the drugs he had and somehow he settled.

When we left it was the kind of beautiful, bright morning that we had no right to expect just as November was about to start. First, we went to visit his parents' grave in Woking. I had been there with him many times before. He had always told us that his parents were an ever-present part of his life.

The cemetery was pristinely kept. The autumnal colours sparkled in the sun. The place had an almost magical feel, and painted a peaceful picture of death. Dad was able to pay there and then to extend his parents' plot for the next twenty-five years and this seemed to take a weight off his mind – he had looked after them for one final time.

The ease with which we discussed Dad's condition shocked the receptionist at the crematorium, I remember. I had once raised the idea of scattering our childhood cat's ashes near Dad's – the idea outraged my sister and amused

Dad, so I quickly backtracked. Characteristically, he took
the chance to wind us up, asking the receptionist whether
they let people scatter their pets' ashes in the garden. No,
she said. 'It's just that I'm on my way out,' he replied, 'and
my daughter wants to mix my ashes with those of her cat.'
She very coolly told us there was a waiting room round
the back that we could sit in – the very clear subtext
being, can I get this insane family away from me? I will
never forget sitting in that funny little room, all three of us
crying with laughter.

He kept repeating how happy he was. He said afterwards
to me that he had a strong sense that day of how much
energy and power we had and that he had felt confident
that this was our time and that we would be all right without him. But I did not feel that then. I was just trying to
ask all the questions I could, to drink in the time.

We drove along the street he grew up on and he told us
about how he started the branch Labour party and
recruited so few people his father had joined just to beef
up the numbers. He told us about how he would knock
on doors along these suburban streets and feel frustrated
that these people's hopes and aspirations were being
ignored by the party he loved.

   He told us about how he found a bigger world in lit-
erature and how something inside him had pushed him to
leave Woking at the age of sixteen. He was anxious for us

to see and understand every detail, that there should be nothing we did not understand.

He showed us the hills he used to struggle up doing his paper round and the construction site he had worked at during the summer holidays. He took us to the woods he used to walk through alone and the rivers he would fish and where he found peace in his own thoughts.

By now the weather had changed. It was pouring with rain by the time we got to Knaphill School, the primary where his dad had been the head teacher, but he insisted on getting out and showing us around, despite our warnings about what Mum would say.

He told us how his dad really cared about the ordinary kids who went there and fought to build them a swimming pool. He reminded us how he had himself struggled at school, how he had been so petrified at his eleven-plus he could hardly write and had ended up at the secondary modern.

We took many photos, printing memories as we went. We had lunch at a pub, where he managed a couple of spoonfuls of soup but insisted we all had three courses.

I can still see him there, beaming at us, happy in the moment.

That was Thursday. By the following Monday, his breathing had become a problem. Breathlessness was a new symptom for him so it had all of us worried, especially

Mum. She always had a sense of when things were really bad. I think so much of his pain and his fear, so many of the demons, became apparent at night.

He had a routine chemotherapy appointment on Tuesday and Mum was so worried she covertly called the hospital, asking for Dad to have some tests as soon as he arrived. They were both stressed and tense that morning and I had a sense of foreboding that whole day.

I was in a meeting when I got a text from Mum at about four saying the doctors thought Dad had a 'bit of pneumonia but was doing OK'. Having learnt with my parents always to add at least 20 per cent to any bad news, I jumped straight into a cab.

When I got to the hospital the atmosphere was tense. I could tell that both my parents were scared but were trying to be strong for each other. Dad was joking away as ever, getting me to massage his neck, interested in my day. It felt like the moment of calm before a storm, waiting for what was going to hit us.

And then very quickly the storm was upon us.

A doctor came in saying she was finishing up before her shift ended and had just come to give us the results of the scan Dad had undergone. He did have an infection, she said, it was on the lungs and was very far advanced. But they were trying to fight it.

There was something in the tone of her voice and the way she would not quite meet our eyes that betrayed the seriousness of the situation. I remember struggling to hold it together.

Dad asked very calmly: 'Is this life-threatening?'

'Yes.'

'Could it be tonight?'

'Yes.'

And suddenly the ground disappeared from beneath our feet.

We had been discussing that Sunday whether Dad would be with us at Christmas and had been making plans for the next few weeks. None of us had thought it could be so quick.

Least of all Dad. There was so much he still wanted to do. I could almost see him running through the list in his mind – the people he wanted to see, the book he planned to finish. His breathing was getting faster and faster as the panic began to set in.

The doctor told us later that Dad's shortness of breath when he walked into his appointment that morning would have hospitalised most people and it was starting to hit him now. Dad told Mum to go and call Professor Cunningham. His voice was strained and I remember frantically trying to find the number, my brain suddenly no longer really connected to my body.

Professor Cunningham told Mum he had seen the scan and that the situation was bad. Get the girls in, he advised, it could be tonight. When Mum left the room

Dad said he could feel that he was dying, that he did not have long left.

I could see him trying to control his panic, trying to keep calm, but he could not quite get a hold on himself. He had said to all of us, and especially to Mum, that his greatest fear of dying from oesophageal cancer was not being able to breathe. He had always had a fear of tight spaces, of drowning – he hated the idea of gasping for breath. He associated breathlessness with the rattle of his father's chest on his deathbed. And at that awful moment it seemed he might get the death he feared rather than the one he wanted.

Dr Craig Carr, the head of the Marsden's intensive care unit, came to talk to us. He was one of those doctors who exudes reassurance and calm and we began to refer to him privately as Smiling Buddha. He repeated that the situation was serious and the infection was very far advanced.

He gave us three options. The first was to do nothing, which would almost certainly mean Dad would not last the night. The second was to support Dad's breathing through an oxygen helmet while they tried to control the infection. Finally, they could make an intervention and put him on a life-support machine, but the chances of him ever coming out of it were very slim.

Dad was slightly calmer now, given some control of his own destiny. He was very clear that he did not want the third option. He did want to live, but not at any cost. He said to Dr Carr that he was going to die anyway and he did not want it to be in terrible pain and discomfort.

Dr Carr left saying he would prepare intensive care and someone would be up to transport Dad shortly. Mum had texted my sister: Get here, now. Grace was already on her way and arrived shortly afterwards, face strained, not wanting to ask too many questions. She later told me she could feel the tension and fear in the room, that it was oppressive.

Dad asked to have a moment alone with each of us. Grace said she kept telling him not to be scared. He told her he was not, but his eyes betrayed him. I told him that he had done enough, written enough; we could take it from here. I tried to let him know how much I loved him but could not find the right words.

I did not want it to be like this. I was not ready. He was not ready. I had so much to say to him, I wanted so much to give voice to the overwhelming strength of my love for him. I wanted to leave nothing unsaid. But this was all too rushed, too brief, and it left me feeling desperate for just a little more time.

The team came up to wheel him down and we took the stairs to wait in the little family room. Grace made us all hot chocolate. None of us said very much.

The nurse eventually called us in to see him. He was lying on a bed in the middle of a small room underneath a canopy of medical equipment. They had put the helmet on him, a clear bag made from thick plastic. It was hooked up to an oxygen machine that was building pressure around his head to aid his breathing.

He looked like something from a comic book. We all laughed and it broke some of the tension. Somehow it seemed appropriate that Dad, who was always so irreverent and could bring humour to any situation, would end up within this rather comical medical invention. There was a little flap that could be opened to give him water or wipe his face, but the helmet stayed on the whole time.

The room was one of a row of private rooms reserved for patients with infections or at risk of an infection. It was a very plain, clinical space – a sink, a couple of chairs, two small windows at the back. Dad faced away from these. There were two screens monitoring his vital signs, one above his bed and one, more detailed, that the nurse watched continuously. So much about this room was reassuring: the constant presence of a nurse, the tubes and wires connecting him to the drugs he needed.

After seeing Dad sitting scared and breathless with no support, intensive care represented security. His breathing settled and about midnight Dr Carr came in and said Dad would definitely live through the night. And he was himself again; as his breathing calmed, so did he.

Dad was now very keen that Mum should get some sleep. She had been up all night with him for the last few days. But I felt he did not want to be on his own, so I said I would stay at the hospital. I could tell Mum and Grace did not want to leave but I pushed them out, saying I would sleep in and they could come first thing.

So I sat with Dad. We looked up the latest polls on the RealClearPolitics website, and debated the fight for the Republican nomination as we had done a million times before.

I put on an episode of *CSI*, the programme he often watched late at night to help shut out the pain. The rest of us really hated it. I have the clearest memory of him getting me to adjust the television, worried that I could not see it properly. Grace later said he did the same with her when she stayed. That little gesture was so typical – despite his pain and discomfort, everything he had been through, it still really mattered to him that I should be able to see the programme properly.

Eventually, in the early hours, he said he wanted to try to sleep. I booked a taxi and cried the whole way home.

Wednesday, 2 November

Mum wanted a bit of time alone with Dad to talk things through so I slept for a couple of hours, until about seven. I woke up with a flashback to the panic of the night before, and called the hospital immediately to check Dad was OK. I was reassured to hear from the nurse that he was feeling fine. Grace and I went in for about eight, picking up breakfast – porridge and coffee – for Mum on the way.

We brought with us some things Dad wanted: his books on dying, his cancer articles, his laptop. Thus began an endless stream of requests from him, made and then instantly forgotten, so the room was full of his jumbled possessions. And somehow this sterile hospital environment became our space. We came and went as we pleased, no one ever asked us to leave and there were no visiting hours. The medical team made us feel part of the hospital. It is strange how quickly you can adjust to a new way of being. This little room became our family home, the new rituals and routines providing a strange sense of comfort and normality.

The medical situation too had become more stable. Dr Carr said Dad would definitely be with us for the next three to five days and we would know by the weekend if the infection was going to turn. If it did, it could still be weeks. Dad asked: 'Can you guarantee me I'll be here in a week?' Dr Carr said no, but 'I can guarantee you that you'll be looked after like a member of my own family.' And he was.

So there was hope. But, as Mum said to me afterwards, in another way there was no hope. We always knew the chances were slim and even if he did recover, this would happen again in a few weeks. I am not sure any of us, Dad least of all, believed that he would leave intensive care again.

Alastair Campbell came in to see us on Wednesday morning. He had been on the phone to Mum living through the night with us. And so it was a bit of a shock for him to see Dad sitting up, grinning and joking away. We found it hard to describe how real and close we had been the night before.

It was surreal sitting there with him, chatting about France, football, Alastair's boys, politics. Dad said to Alastair, 'You know, you've lived your whole life wanting to live in an invisible bubble, now I'm in a real one.' Alastair was running a quiz that night and tested out the questions on us. James, the day nurse, joined in. We could have been in our sitting room at home.

Alastair wrote in his diary after he left:

PG still with us. They had stabilised him and he said I should go in later. He was in bed ten on the intensive care unit. Gail and the girls there. A nice nurse called James who was a big Norwich fan. PG had his head inside a plastic bubble which was helping him to breathe. He had tubes galore into one hand and arm. Yet he was so much better than I had expected. Chatty, funny, and apart from when he moved, and lost his breath, generally ok. I said never do that to me again. What? Make me feel you're dead when you're not. But when the girls went to get a cup of tea, he said he was still looking at days not weeks. I stayed for an hour or so and it was at times almost as though he wasn't really dying. Like any other chat. But not for the first time when I left I wondered if it was the last time I would see him. I did a bit of work when I got home, blogged again on Greece, did a bit of a bike session but I was feeling very down and anxious about him. I had to go out later and host the Portland pub quiz which was fine. Lifted me out of the gloom but I was straight back in on the way home.

After he left we all sat round chatting, laughing and planning. We had never been closer than we were that day. Dad kept saying, 'We have a great family, all here together.' He would look around at us all, grinning. He loved it when we were all up, when we were close.

And Mum was at the heart of this. I always knew she was strong – as Dad used to say, she was a force of nature. But somehow she rose to that moment. She had endless love and comfort for Grace and me and she was Dad's pillar of strength. As his body slowly started to fail she became his extra limbs. He was never really calm unless she was in the room. He looked to her for help with the doctors, trusted her to be his voice when he did not have one. It was like the strength of her love suddenly gave her this extra power, it was extraordinary. And at the same time she let herself lean on Grace and me more than she ever had done before. We just became a total team.

Dad seemed to me to be working on two planes. On the deeper internal one, he was coming to terms with the new situation. But, more immediately, he was also dealing with

the limits of his body and a mind slightly befuddled by
drugs. He was often a little high and some of his lines kept
us in hysterics. At one point on Wednesday he looked over
and said, 'Look, there's the new unit over there – the three
Gs. My little Gracie, the fighter, is the left back, Georgia
is Bobby Moore, the heart and soul of the team, and Mum
is Alex Ferguson.'

During the afternoon Grace and I popped out to give my
parents some time together. We had some sushi, feeling
very strange and exposed outside the hospital. We bought
Dad a little lion and a card saying 'Daddy of all Daddies',
writing one line each. We found him a Dictaphone, to add
to the pile of possessions he never used.

I remember announcing in the evening that this was the
happiest day of my life and my family all looked at me like
I had lost the plot. But it was true.

We had returned from that point of absolute haunting
fear. Dad had been saying for a while how when you are
given a definite deadline, time loses its meaning. When
you are not planning for tomorrow, time becomes circu-
lar and all you have is the moment. So the moment goes
on for ever.

When he said it I remember thinking: time does not
stand still for the rest of us, Dad – we have to imagine a
future without you. I thought about the election campaigns
he would miss, the boyfriends he would never meet, the

children he would not know. But somehow that moment on Tuesday night, when we all faced death together, had changed everything.

Those last few days were the longest of my life. Every conversation, every smile took on a new significance. I felt the most pain and the most joy I have ever felt. And sitting there on Wednesday I felt so incredibly lucky to have those few days, and I knew Dad did too. He looked at the time he had left, recalculated, and thought, yeah, that is just enough. Just enough time to say goodbye, to finish my book, to get things right.

He was a strategist; he wanted to have some control over his destiny, to choose his death. He drank in knowledge about his condition. He had no interest in being distracted from what was happening or hiding in escapism. He was constantly aware, asking questions, analysing and re-analysing his situation. And in his final days he watched his numbers constantly, as if his charts were an exit poll – what are my numbers today?

There is no doubt that he did not want to die. That he had so much more he wanted to give, to do. He loved life so fully and deeply. When I chose the poem I would read at his funeral, 'Because I have loved life, I shall have no sorrow to die' ('A Song of Living' by Amelia Josephine Burr), it summed him up for me.

This was not the peaceful end of someone who thought they had given everything they had to give. He appreciated the intensity of the Death Zone, as he called it, because he was someone who loved life. He found a way to reconcile the two, empowering himself in facing death by making the life he had left count.

He looked at us and said:

'Girls, four days left to try and change the world. You can do a lot in four days.'

The three of us left that night together at about eleven after he had fallen asleep, exhausted but a lot happier. The house felt very empty and we all floated about a bit, struggling to sleep.

Thursday, 3 November

On Thursday, Grace and Mum got to the hospital very early. Grace had to leave in a couple of hours for a work shift and Dad had visits from Matthew Freud and Professor Cunningham. By the time I came in mid-morning, Mum was sitting working away on her BlackBerry and Dad was resting, exhausted from a busy morning. Mum never stopped working, finding an hour here and there when Dad was sleeping, still on top of things even when her life was falling apart around her.

Dad had a long conversation with Matthew and I knew that meant a lot to him. Dad loved Matthew like he was family.

*

Mum told me Dad had been telling Professor Cunning-ham that he knew he was approaching death because of the dreams he had started to have. They were intense, extraordinary dreams like nothing he had ever experi-enced. He would be overwhelmed by the richness of what he saw − a beautiful city, just out of reach, made up of a kaleidoscope of colours, paintings, tapestries and buildings. This would be interspersed with periods of blackness. Somehow he felt death was calling him.

I came in with an article I had written for our local paper and Dad immediately perked up. He was always our biggest fan, so proud of our achievements, dismissing our failures as learning experiences. He spent about forty min-utes carefully struggling through the article. By then his breathing was declining even with the machine's support and we were trying to stop him speaking so much. But he kept telling anyone who came in, this is my daughter, this is her article.

I left the room so the nurses could help him off the bed on to the chair. When I came back in he was very proud of himself, told me he had made a funny joke. As he had got up, wearing his bubble helmet, he said: 'One small step for man.' He kept laughing at his spaceman analogy. He spent so much of his last few days smiling and laughing, his hap-piness lifting all of us. He was in so much pain and discomfort but somehow his spirit took him beyond that.

Mum had to go out for a meeting so I spent a difficult couple of hours with him. His helmet kept leaking air, drooping round his face, making him claustrophobic. At the same time, without the extra pressure he was instantly short of breath. It just kept happening, and I watched the stress grow in his expression each time as his numbers dropped, try though he did to suppress it.

But he had a wonderful nurse who kept him calm, coaxed him through and eventually helped him rest. While he was sleeping she filled up the noticeboard, wanting to know his likes and dislikes. Earlier Dad had announced to the room, 'The love you take is equal to the love you make,' quoting the Beatles' song 'The End' on *Abbey Road*. So she wrote that up as his motto of the day.

There was a constant stream of nurses who took care of Dad and they were all very different. I remember him writing that cancer had changed his view of leadership, that he had been sustained time and time again on his cancer journey by strength in extraordinary places. And not one nurse we met in that week failed to live up to this. They all worked long hours without ever showing a lapse in concentration. They were always ready with a smile, a word of comfort, and they made us feel totally at home. We met so many different people but everyone seemed somehow familiar. There seemed to be an army of people looking out for him. They were as worried about his needs as we were – whether he wanted his glasses on or off, how he was breathing. Eventually they even constructed a little straw so he could drink without losing air.

Overseeing it all was Dr Carr, the head of the intensive care unit, who never seemed to leave or sleep. He was the absolute best of the NHS, he gave the whole family so much reassurance and somehow he made what should have been the worst five days of our life bearable. I know Dad loved the camaraderie of the medical staff; he always took energy from other people and he felt comforted by the constant security. The night nurses in particular took him through the darkest hours, in both senses of the term.

That evening the doctors were concerned about Dad's breathing, the strain it was causing, how much he was struggling. I could sense the evening nurse's extra watch-fulness and anxiety and it was decided to up the support he was getting from the helmet to 100 per cent. This was as much as they could do to help him, yet it was clear that he was not improving. There was still a vague hope that the situation would turn, but it was fading fast.

Grace came back after work and was very low. She says she remembers Dad looking at her.

'What's wrong, little Gracie?'

'What do you *think* is wrong, Dad?'

Grace and I went to get some food for dinner and, in our exhaustion, started squabbling when it took ages to arrive.

It was always worse when you left the hospital. The uncertainty left you feeling constantly on edge. Any beep of the phone filled you with total dread. Mum and Grace would answer the phone in the same rushed, urgent tone: 'What's happened?' I knew I did the same thing. It was much calmer in the room, watching the machine, knowing what was happening.

Dad was exhausted and slept through most of the evening. Thursday had been a tougher day and we were starting to prepare again for bad news.

Mum later said there was a paradox to Dad in those final days. There is no doubt he had moments of fear and uncertainty. He was battling against death to the end. But fundamentally he accepted what was happening to him, faced up to what was coming with composure. Feeling empowered was essential to him. He had a tranquilliser that he hid in one of his books and this became his comfort blanket. It was always near him. By the end there was no way he could have taken it alone, but somehow it gave him protection from the forces ranged against him. It helped him stay calm.

Friday, 4 November

Friday morning Mum had gone in very early to catch Dr Carr on his rounds. He made it clear to her that it was definitely three to five days now and that the infection was not going to turn. I remember coming in just afterwards and Dad worrying if Mum had told me, but she did not have to say anything. I already knew he was deteriorating.

I had gone shopping to get him some lime cordial and ice and he was delighted. He kept saying it was the best thing he had ever tasted. After every sip of cold water he would close his eyes and smile with a look of total contentment.

Mum was in tears at lunch as she worried about the time after the ordeal ended. I told her we would get through it together, walk through the pain, have good days and bad. I remember holding her hand, feeling helpless, knowing there was no real comfort for any of us.

Adrian Steirn's team came by with ten copies of the pictures they had taken of Dad standing defiantly on his grave. They wanted him to sign them. They asked tentatively if they could take pictures of him doing it. It was strange to see their evident shock and distress at how he looked. To me, it had become familiar.

He struggled to sign the pictures, getting me to test the pens, frustrated that his body would not respond to his wishes. He exhausted himself in the process. I could feel Mum worrying and thinking: even now he won't stop. Dad was proudly telling all the staff that the picture was taken at Highgate Cemetery where his ashes would be scattered. The nurses looked utterly bemused by the whole thing.

Grace came in a bit later and his eyes lit up. Grace always had the capacity to make Dad laugh, to say something unexpected, to distract him. He tried to kiss her head, looking confused as he realised the bubble was in the way. We all laughed.

Grace and I went for the daily dinner run and he looked at us both as if for the last time, squeezing my hand with such love. He started: 'I know I won't be there for the big moments . . .' We both instantly burst into tears. He knew how to get us, loved grand statements. He told us he would always be with us really. That he loved us so much. That this was our moment, that we were on the cusp, were ready to shine, to explode. He told us to believe in ourselves, that we were both stars. He said his mum on her deathbed had told him to look after his dad but that he did not need to tell us to look after Mum. He knew we would.

When we came back he was trying to type, struggling to lift his arms. We tried to prop him up with pillows but he would not let us help. He sat there for what seemed like hours but only got a few words down, telling me 'I'm away with the typing, George.' That was when I really broke down, hiding behind his bed, silently crying. I could not bear to see his body letting him down. Eventually he fell asleep in front of his computer.

I could see Mum was shattered but would never leave on her own, so I said I would take her home and that Grace would stay. Grace was delighted to have some time alone with Dad, and had hated having to go into work.

As we left, Dad was struggling with his phone. He could not type in the password and asked us to remove it. We tried but failed, accidently changing it in the process. We wrote out the new one for him in massive letters but he looked at us with disdain. The drugs were starting to have a big effect and he was getting a bit confused, but every time he felt we were even remotely patronising he would cut us down to size very quickly. He had lost a bit of clarity, but his mind was so strong and he was always very much present.

I remember that night knowing things were getting worse, feeling that a deep sadness had opened like an abyss in my chest and would never close. But I also felt a profound sense of joy and warmth as I ran over every tiny memory from that day, basking in each.

Saturday, 5 November

We all go in very early. Dad asks how many days he has left, counting them down. He thinks the worst-case scenario is three. We break it to him that three was yesterday, now it is only two. We can see his disappointment and frustration as he realises it is one less than he thought. He wants more time.

He waits until Mum is out of the room and tells me to sort out his papers, to make sure his book gets finished and to get Labour people to the funeral. He wants the church to be packed, and tells me I should get Margaret McDonagh on it.

His sister, Jill, comes by and they spend some time alone together, saying goodbye. They have both been very independent spirits, following their own paths, but I know the closeness between them in his final months was one of his greatest comforts. She is a Church of England priest so is able to give him a religious blessing.

Afterwards Grace sits helping him text, his coordination so bad that communication has become increasingly erratic. We catch him trying to send Ed Victor a text saying 'These are the best of times, these are the worst of times'; I am not sure he even realises he is channelling Dickens. Alastair later describes a confused message from Peter Hyman asking why Dad has emailed him saying nothing but '3–5 days'.

And then suddenly he becomes very focused and determined.

He knows time is slipping away faster now and he has to take his opportunity. The big thing hanging over him is the book. He believes that the common narrative on death is wrong, that dying can be a time of profound growth and happiness. He is desperate to articulate this, to get his thoughts down on paper.

He tries to type, gets nowhere, so begins to dictate to Mum. And it is torture. Mum is helping because it is so important to him but she hates every second of it, knowing he is doing himself so much damage. Grace notes his almost possessed look, eyes half-open and red, voice rasping. He speaks and speaks. Mum fills the pages. He has gone deep inside himself.

I feel intolerable pain as I listen to him struggle to get his words out, his voice a low murmuring grumble.

When it comes down to it, it is not enough for Dad just to have his family around him, though I know it means the world to him. The most important thing to him is his drive, his purpose, his desire to give meaning to the experience of dying. That is why the book means so much to him. And so he digs somewhere deep, beyond his body, for his final spark of energy and reserves to write his parting thoughts. He has been too sick for weeks to do this but somehow he knows it is now or never. He is facing death by fighting with all he has to find meaning in it.

The doctor comes in worried about Dad's numbers and tells him he has to stop talking, but Dad is determined.

We have told only a handful of people so far, not wanting to force all his friends to live through this with us. But now I think there are some who have to know. I step out to call Pete, his oldest friend from university, who now lives in Boston, Massachusetts. When he answers he says: 'Georgia, don't say anything. I'm on the top of a ladder.' He comes down and I tell him what is happening. I hear the shock in his voice. Like all of us, he had thought there would be more time.

And still Dad talks. Finally he comes to the end and he is so relieved, looking for our praise. He keeps repeating the phrase 'fought hard today'. We want him to calm down.

Queens Park Rangers are about to kick off against Manchester City. I get the match up on Sky Sports. Dad and I have been QPR season-ticket holders since I was six and have travelled together around the country to watch them.

He gets very excited – 'Look, it's Neil Warnock' – and wants to know why the quality of the picture is so much better than when we watched games in Newcastle. Mum is slightly disapproving so I ask him if he would prefer some Gregorian chants. He looks at me as if I am insane.

'Georgia, I'm watching the football.'

He keeps trying to lift his arms above his head the way he would do at home. But they are so bloated now, four times their usual size from being attached to all these wires, he cannot quite get them above his bubble hat. It is so sweet, almost comical: such a familiar gesture in this medical world. QPR score an equaliser and his numbers go up.

But he is getting more distressed and his breathing is getting worse, so I turn the game off to try to get him to rest. And so he does not see us lose.

Alastair sends Dad the most beautiful letter. So we read it to him, all in floods of tears, and he, calm as anything, jabs at the laptop screen and says 'Funeral, funeral.'

He tells us his breathing is getting more difficult now and the nurse ups his sedatives. He suddenly announces, 'I'm done,' and we all get a bit panicked. But then he says, 'I'm done. I've finished the book.'

He makes a gasping sound like he is trying to catch the air. Grace and Mum stand on one side hugging each other, Grace's eyes big and bright from crying, Mum looking at Dad with such tenderness.

He slips into a dazed sleep, then wakes up a bit confused and says, 'Breathing hard now, breathing a problem, I want to crash out.' He is not petrified like before. He has steadied himself. He is ready. He looks around and cannot see me on his other side.

'Where's Georgia?'

'Here, Dad,' I say.

He grabs my hand so tightly and tells us to sort out 'The Glory of the Ride', meaning this book. He says 'Goodnight, love you,' to each of us in turn. He falls into a light sleep, wakes up, and does the whole thing again.

He is very insistent that it is time for us to go to bed,

that we need to get a taxi home. He calls out to the nurse on duty, 'Ebony, put me to bed now.' We say, 'Dad, you are in bed,' but he barely hears us.

His last words are: 'I'm going to crash out now, I'm done.'

And he falls into a deep sleep.

Is he scared? How much does he know? I cannot know for sure, but I remember Alastair, years ago at a Labour Party event, reading a quote from an American football coach: 'I firmly believe that any man's finest hour, the greatest fulfilment of all that he holds dear, is that moment when he has worked his heart out in a good cause and lies exhausted on the field of battle — victorious.' And I feel that is where Dad is at this moment.

He has fought as hard as he can. He has the people he loves around him and he is ready to fall into his dreams.

Later, Mum, tears rolling down her face, reads to us Dylan Thomas's poem, 'Do not go gentle into that good night . . . rage, rage against the dying of the light.' In the end he is not going gently. He is going the way he has lived, with determination, purpose and resolve, fighting to make every second count.

The nurse tells us that it would be better if we stayed the night, so when it is clear he is fast asleep we move to the little relatives' room next door. The nurses promise to call if anything happens.

Grace and I run home to grab some spare clothes and wash stuff. Before I go I tell Mum it is time to let people know what is happening. She composes a beautiful email and we send it to an old mailing list, not really sure who is or is not on it.

Sunday, 6 November

We rest on an improvised construction of sofa beds and pillows. I barely sleep, waking at around four in the morning. I must have been making a lot of noise because Mum very drily suggests that I go and sit with Dad.

So I do, sitting with him and the nurse, listening to Bob Marley gently playing in the background. The nurse has taken a lot of care to get him comfortable, tidy up his tubes. He looks well but firmly asleep. She says she stopped giving him sedatives at about midnight.

Grace and Mum come through an hour later and we all sit around him, not really sure why he is not waking up. His breathing seems strong and his numbers are fine.

Eventually a young doctor comes by on his rounds. He asks us if Dad was talking a lot yesterday. And we say yes, all day. The doctor describes how the effort of speaking emitted so much carbon dioxide into his blood that Dad created a natural sedative, gassing himself into unconsciousness. 'Like if you gas yourself in a car?' Mum asks, incredulous.

'Exactly,' he says.

The doctor tells us it is extremely unlikely that Dad will wake up now, but he cannot say how long he will stay like this. It could be hours, it could be days. It is not a shock to us and in a way there is a real beauty to it. Through his relentless search for purpose he has given himself the peaceful, natural death he craves. He is, in the end, the master of his own destiny.

Grace and I sit, having tea, still coming to terms with the fact we will never speak to him again. Suddenly Grace says: 'You know what Dad would have said then, don't you? He would have said, "That's exactly the kind of man you should marry, Georgia".' And we both break into laughter. It is his classic line. No one tells you how precious and powerful moments of happiness and connection are when you are living through a nightmare.

The three of us spend the rest of the day at his side. I put on the Gregorian chants he always uses for meditation, infusing the room with a peaceful, almost spiritual atmosphere. The nurse leaves to sit outside. There is nothing she can do now. The rounds stop. Much of the medical equipment is gone. This is a time for peace and goodbyes.

Alastair and Fiona visit. He hugs us, seeming incredibly solid. Fiona says Dad was a life force, that he has given us all so much, that we are three amazing women.

Tony arrives and hugs us all warmly. We tell him about

the few days in hospital, Dad's final purpose. We tell him that Dad had known he was coming in and had been looking forward to it. We leave him alone with Dad to say goodbye. He leaves at about twelve, taking some time to speak to all the staff.

Ebony, his nurse from the night before, comes to say goodbye at the end of her shift. She says she has only known him for a few hours but that she thinks he is a remarkable person – so kind and polite even as he faces the end, and that he has so much zest for life.

He seems so strong lying there, the sound of his breathing mixing with the chanting and filling the room. I feel I could hold his hand for ever, as long as he stays with us. I can feel how strong and warm he is, his skin papery smooth. His hand is like a testament to the person he used to be – so disconnected from the rest of him, his shoulders and knees thin and wasted, his arms bloated now beyond recognition.

Dr Carr comes in and tells us that they can give him the 'Michael Jackson' drug, which is a sedative that can give wonderful dreams. We are very worried about him waking up and being scared, so we agree that sounds perfect. He says they will gradually lower the pressure and take off the helmet so he is breathing more naturally. We know now there is not long left. So we talk to him about good times, holidays, places he loves, moments we treasure, hoping it helps his dreams.

Matthew Freud silently slips in, standing with us, part of the family. He has some time alone with Dad and leaves at about five, tears in his eyes.

The staff take off the helmet and Dad instantly looks far more fragile. His breathing, rasping and shallow now, comes in short, sharp intakes.

We read him the messages coming through from his friends, hoping he can hear. We read some poetry from a book someone bought us about grief, somehow giving voice to our feelings. We take turns to break down, then to be strong for each other, like dominoes falling.

At about seven in the evening, David Cunningham visits. He has been there for the whole journey and it feels right that he is here at the end. He tells us he has seen a lot of death, probably too much, but he has never seen anything like Dad.

He has always thought Dad is a great man but in August, when he was given the terminal diagnosis, he had really seen what an amazing person he is. All the way through Dad has never shied away from what is happening, has accepted it and faced it. Most people, he said, could not do that, let alone have the ability to give it a voice, describe it. Dad has done a lot of great things in his life, he says, but this is the greatest. He has changed a lot of people, changed him, through his positivity and strength.

*

And finally it is just the four of us.

I am holding on to his left hand, Grace his right. Mum has her arm around his neck, leaning on his chest. The Gregorian chant fills the room and as it reaches its last note, Dad gives a shudder and lets go.

And the room is for a microsecond full of a powerful energy. Mum feels a flash of joy. She is sobbing, overcome, repeating in awe: 'Philip, I didn't know it would be so beautiful.'

I feel as if a huge part of me has been wrenched out. Grace manages to go and get the doctor.

The life drains from him very quickly. The warmth, the colour, the rhythm of his breathing disappears. In seconds his body is cold, chalky white. And there is no doubt he is gone. What is left is a shell and no longer even really looks like him. The difference between even a thread of life and death is immeasurable. The love, the passion, the spirit that defined him is somewhere else now.

We kiss his forehead one last time: not wanting to leave, unable to stay. But as we walk out of the intensive care unit, our only comfort is that he has had the death he wanted, at peace and surrounded by his family.

My Dad

Grace Gould

When I was younger Dad was an enigma to me. He was an exotic treat who would come and go, bringing us various trinkets and political-slogan T-shirts from his travels. He would come in, slam the door, and his energy would lift the house. On holiday we would cherish him. We would play games, hide Georgia's teddy bears, devise elaborate adventures and cause Mum all sorts of anxiety.

After 2005 Dad changed. He returned home and became more grounded in our lives. For Dad and me this marked the beginning of a friendship. We divided life into two categories: things that amused us and things that did not.

Georgia's boyfriends occupied the former and everything in the latter was often ignored.

We found random topics to obsess over. I taught him to use BBM (the BlackBerry Messenger system) which he came to adore, bombarding me with hilarious stories or Kate Moss gossip.

He would come with me to obscure environmental conferences. We would go to the cinema and eat vegan Chinese takeouts at four in the afternoon. The funniest adventure was when Dad came with me to Glastonbury, in a purpose-bought parka. He camped for one night then booked into the nearest hotel.

Of course these years coincided with me being a horrendous teenager and I am sure these fads formed part of a Yoda-like strategy to bond with a younger daughter who could not name more than three Cabinet members, let alone a QPR player. But he made it work and we found our way to relate.

When Dad became ill he changed once again. He mellowed, his energy shifted from an over-excited bustle to quiet force. He channelled his intensity first into staying alive and then into learning how to die. Our relationship shifted too. Our irreverence for life was now directed at cancer.

I felt that during this time Dad and I became much closer. We spoke candidly about his death, his funeral, our future without him. He would talk about his insecurities, symptoms and fears. And when the time was right – and more often when it was not – we would descend into the ridiculous, joking about all the absurdities that came with cancer.

I do not think that I am the only person slightly terrified about how to live without Dad. He was the first port of call for so many. At Dad's funeral, his close friend Noreena described how he used to sit holding court, with a constant stream of people coming to visit him for advice. Although I would never have dreamt of saying this to Dad when he was alive, he did have a fantastic gift for knowing what was going on, telling you what you should do and then reassuring you that if you did it, then everything would be OK.

Before he went to Newcastle he wrote Georgia and me each a letter to be opened only after his death, and gave us five rules for life. In his letter to me, he wrote:

> I know that you want me to answer every question that the future holds but I can't do that. Or at least I cannot do that in the way you wanted. What I can say is this: if you are yourself, if you trust yourself, if you believe in yourself your life will be fine. As for the rest of it: be generous and warm-hearted and always send a thank-you card. This is all you need to know. And if you get really stuck ask Matthew, and if he can't help, ask the universe. The answer is out there and I promise you, you will find it.

Postscript

Gail Rebuck

Philip had never been ill. It was as if focus and determination rode roughshod over mere physical problems. That did not stop him from keeping a complete pharmacy at home for every eventuality. Paradoxically, he constantly worried he was ill, but he never was ill. It was not until we went on holiday to Brazil for Christmas 2007, when his indigestion and swallowing problems became more pronounced, that I thought for the first time maybe something was truly wrong.

He had some tests when we were back in London and they seemed to be fine, but then one night he suddenly woke at 3 a.m. feeling very ill. He was as white as a sheet and in a panic, so I called an ambulance thinking he was having a heart attack. We arrived at University College Hospital and went straight into the emergency room but they could not find anything wrong with his heart. We finally put the episode down to dehydration rather than the massive tumour that was growing at the junction of his oesophagus and stomach.

Looking back at Philip's cancer over four years is like looking at a series of stills – moments of intensity, worry and readjustment. When I went to collect him from the endoscopy he was lying flat, looking ashen. He said simply: 'It's cancer and it's bad.' The doctor gave him a 50 per cent chance of surviving.

The world really did change in that second and for me it was a moment of total panic. I had never heard of oesophageal cancer, had no idea it had reached epidemic levels and that the chances of a cure without surgery were non-existent. I remember running through the hospital to find the surgeon who had been called in to look at the tumour and pleading with his assistant to get us back in to see him the next day.

This first stage was one of confusion, shock and the desperate search for information. We knew we faced three months of chemotherapy, but this was all by way of a dress rehearsal for the operation, which would be a stark kill or cure.

The choice of surgeon and hospital was the most crucial decision we had to make. In a sense the luxury of having that choice was our undoing. Had we gone to our local hospital and had a radical oesophagectomy, it is possible that Philip would be alive today.

If we had known about Professor Mike Griffin's world-class unit in Newcastle, things might have been different. But there was no information on centres of excellence in the UK and most of the senior health practitioners and government officials we consulted pointed us towards America.

Philip was very keen on going to the United States. I was less keen, not for medical reasons but because of the practicalities of recovering from such a major operation without the support of nearby family and friends. But after an exploratory trip, America prevailed.

You could not fail to be impressed by the sheer scale of the Memorial Sloan-Kettering Cancer Center and its depth of experience. But when Philip walked into the operating theatre, I had to sit for seven hours in the coffee shop without any information or update. It was the longest seven hours of my life. I tried to calm my nerves by visiting each of the main religious meditation centres dotted around the hospital but all I could do was imagine the worst.

Eventually, I was told the operation was over and that Philip was OK. Like Dante's circles of hell, in reverse order, I was moved to a waiting area outside intensive care for a couple of hours until the surgeon was ready to see me.

Murray Brennan looked exhausted, his overalls spattered with blood. The operation had been a success but he had had trouble reattaching what was left of Philip's stomach. He said that towards the end he thought he would have to break Philip's ribs and make another incision to complete the join, but he eventually managed the less traumatic operation he had intended. Something in his hesitancy worried me. I never told Philip about it but, of course, the tumour regrew in exactly that spot.

I went in to see Philip, who was in remarkably good form, full of drugs and relief, wanting to call the girls in London. They were so happy that we all just broke down together as the tension of the last twenty-four hours eased. The next day, however, he was as white as a corpse, in terrible discomfort, in a tiny room, separated from the next bed by a thin curtain and unable to speak. Everything was a battle and it was taking place on unfamiliar territory.

Although Philip slowly recovered and even started eating small amounts, one of his stitches became infected. As the hospital did not favour the use of antibiotics, for fear of MRSA, they left the wound open. And that is how it remained – a great gaping gash that turned into a massive hernia as eventually it healed – a ghastly reminder of what had been and how far we still had to go.

But the pathology was good and I still have the

congratulatory messages on my phone from the medics in
the UK saying this was all behind us now.

I look back at that period in New York and wonder how
we all coped with it – the girls at university, Georgia doing
her finals and Grace in her first year. I was working from
our New York office where Random House had given me
all the support I needed to carry on with my day job
between hospital visits. My friend Ed Victor used to say
that once diagnosed you inhabit Planet Cancer. Philip's
cancer was the new focus of my life – a long strip of land
around which family and work forked and flowed like a
river on either side.

We returned to London to more chemotherapy and,
thank goodness, we discovered Professor David Cunningham at the Marsden. Philip has written about this
wonderful hospital but what I experienced there was a
level of intimacy and care that made the whole experience
much more tolerable.

Unfortunately my closest friend had also taken resi-
dence on Planet Cancer and, after an operation for breast
cancer at St Mary's, came to the Marsden for her
chemotherapy. I would wander the hospital between the
two of them, especially at moments of crisis. Philip was
not tolerating his post-operative chemo at all well and my
snapshot of him at that time was sitting with his drip on
an armchair at home concentrating on his BlackBerry,
unable to speak, just holding it together.

My friend tolerated her chemotherapy much better, apart from one ghastly episode when she was hospitalised. I kept Philip and her separate, even though they compared cancer notes on a regular basis, because one day she came over and I caught sight of them together, thin, frail, practically bald. It seemed that the two most important people in my life were going to be taken away and it was unbearable.*

Yet in all this misery there were moments of light. At the end of his post-operative chemotherapy Philip was desperate to get away but as we could not fly we were limited to travelling to Europe by train. It had to be Venice, Philip's favourite city on earth. And it was, as Philip describes it, like moving from the dark to the light.

It was August. We stayed at the Hotel Cipriani for what was probably our most idyllic holiday. Philip kept announcing he could now eat only if he was given brilliantly prepared Italian food. We kept mostly to the hotel, like two inexperienced tourists. One morning over breakfast I noticed a large number of boats bobbing about outside. As we wondered what was going on we noticed George Clooney and Brad Pitt at another table. We had stumbled into the Venice Film Festival.

Life settled into a kind of routine. Venetian food apart, eating was increasingly difficult and mealtimes became

*My friend made a full recovery. People would pay a lot of money for the amazing, full head of platinum-coloured hair she has now.

fraught. I was anxious that Philip get some nutrients while he behaved around food like a truculent teenager.

The other cancer-free holiday we took was in Jordan. This was a real experiment and although I had arranged all sorts of sightseeing, there was no certainty when we started that Philip would be up to any of it. In the end, as we set off to Petra, Philip was concerned about how uncomfortable he would feel on the car journey. He not only made that; overcome by the sheer grandeur of the experience, he also managed the long walk to Al Khazneh (the Treasury), and even insisted on a detour the next day to visit an abandoned Crusader fort.

These were wonderful moments of joy and liberation. It was clear Philip was fundamentally scarred by his experiences but it was as if he was testing his own boundaries, in the hope of living a semblance of a normal life.

And in a way we were closer than ever. We had been through hell together and emerged the other side. We had spent our lives working incredibly hard, living out our different purposes, worrying about the girls as only two working parents can. We always thought there would be a time after work and parenthood when we would live out our old age together. It looked as if cancer would dissolve that future. That Philip had survived seemed a miracle and those holidays were like a blessing. But it was to be all too short.

*

Philip's key moments would often coincide with stress-ful moments in my work life. Work events may seem trivial when compared to matters of life and death, but life flowed on relentlessly either side of Planet Cancer. Although it was sometimes a struggle to fulfil obligations, for most of the time work for me was an oasis of normality.

I arrived in New York just a day before Philip's operation as I had had to go to a meeting in Berlin. And two years later, the day of our appointment at the Marsden in Sutton to get some key test results, I was giving a lunch for an American author, who was in London just for the day and was a little surprised when I left early.

I left that table full of trepidation. The agony of waiting for results is familiar to all on Planet Cancer – and it is a life sentence – but in Philip's case we always sensed when bad news was coming. So it was this time: the cancer was back with a vengeance. All our dreams disappeared that afternoon.

We knew we were running out of options. Philip tried various kinds of chemotherapy but there was very little response. Further surgery was the only option.

At first the Marsden thought we should go back to America to the same surgeon, as he would know his own handiwork. For the first time I put my foot down. I could not face Memorial Sloan-Kettering again, its isolation and organisational challenges, with all the extra complexities this second time around. Although Murray Brennan was up for the second operation, he wanted to do it with a colleague because of its complexity. That worried me too. I didn't feel either of us would get through it again.

I pleaded with David Cunningham that there must be somewhere closer to home. We were going to see one of the Marsden surgeons but Professor Cunningham explained that very few people would be willing to attempt this second operation. Then he mentioned Mike Griffin. Philip explains the long courtship and measured response he found in Newcastle. I went up there to collect Philip from the first of his tests, one of many, many commutes on GNER.

Professor Griffin was upfront and unequivocal – he would do the operation but he wanted me, in particular, to be fully briefed about the risks. I diligently wrote them all down, like a macabre shopping list. Eventually we got the go-ahead. We moved to Newcastle, to a central flat on Grey Street that I teased Philip reminded me of *Footballers' Wives*. The night before the operation we went to dinner down the road and I was so out of sorts I left my handbag in the restaurant.

Another operation, another coffee shop. Worry is like a kettle full of water, it felt as if my mind was on the boil at a ferocious intensity with no opportunity to let off steam. There is nothing you can do but get through it as best you can.

After the operation had been under way for about five hours, I decided to go for a walk. I bumped into Professor Griffin coming out of the operating theatre at the end of round one. It was another gruelling five hours until I saw him again in his little office. The operation had been the kind of success that only a master surgeon could have achieved.

Professor Griffin said that towards the end he had thought of removing all of Philip's stomach and creating a pouch for food out of his colon, but that would have taken another four hours. I could tell he was reflecting on this decision. So I said: 'But when you looked at Philip, as you have looked at thousands before, what was left of his stomach looked in good shape so you decided to leave it there as the best option for the patient. It was a decision you made on the basis of years of experience.'

He replied: 'So you really understand about decisions.'

'Yes I do,' I said, 'but at least mine do not involve life and death. And I think you made the right one.'

I did not tell Philip about that conversation either.

The intensive care experience in the UK was very different from what we had found in New York. Although I had been warned, nothing could have prepared me for the sight of Philip intubated after the operation. He looked like a corpse. The staff were going to keep him under sedation all night so I was told to return early the following morning. When I did, they had removed the tube. But

Philip was barely conscious and clearly in a lot of pain, so I just sat there and tried with little success to interpret what he wanted. I don't know how I held it together – but I tried to be strong for both of us.

Philip writes about the elasticity of time in the Death Zone – how it becomes positively distorted into emotional time. That was also true during and immediately after both his major operations. You only think of getting through the next hour. That hour seamlessly melts into another hour, and so on. Real time and life are suspended since your whole focus is on the patient, as if you could will them better. Rituals also play a part: the walk to the hospital, coffee from the hospital shop, topping up the TV card. The thousand little inconsequential actions that measure out the day.

Everything about Newcastle was solid and reassuring. Philip could not have been in better hands. But when we came in just months later to hear the results of the pathology it was bad news all the way.

This meant radiotherapy back at the Marsden and a feeding tube. How I hated the sound of the feed going in at night – the alarm beeping if it had become disconnected and thick yellow gunge pouring everywhere. But the feeding tube was Philip's lifeline and I guarded it like a precious jewel.

Philip was always almost pulling it out; each day I

examined the stitches that held it in place with tremendous panic.

Life settled down into a pattern of sorts again – me coaxing Philip to take his pills and to eat a little to supplement the tube. I worried about him constantly. Somehow it was easier to worry than to face up to my underlying fear of a life without him.

With his return to a routine, I thought it would be safe to go to the Jerusalem Book Fair, something which I had promised the organiser, Zev Birger, I would do for many years. One of our authors, Ian McEwan, had been invited to receive an award and that decided me. I left Philip with Georgia and Grace, and a nurse, and set off. I was sitting on the plane when Philip called and told me not to panic – never a good sign. He had pulled out the feeding tube and he and Georgia were at UCH, with Newcastle explaining what had to be done. If you fed a tube back into the channels left by the old one within hours, they were told, it would avoid another operation, and a great Italian emergency care doctor was able to do just that. But I worried all the way to Jerusalem.

The tube became a feature of our lives for several months, with many trips to UCH, until after the radiotherapy when Philip pulled it out once and for all.

Thanks to the medical staff in Newcastle we had a year that would otherwise not have happened. We even

managed a summer holiday in Italy, staying in two extraordinary hotels, a dream of Philip's for many summers. But
all was not well. When you live close to illness, sometimes
it takes a change of scenery to notice changes closer to
home.

Philip did eat for the first week but he was getting thinner. He was almost skeletal. The second week he could
hardly keep any food down and I was almost relieved that
he spent all his time finishing off the update of *The
Unfinished Revolution*, sometimes trying to work alongside
me in a flurry of papers. I knew he was very ill, but there
would be a time and a place to face all that.

When we arrived home, the tumour markers exploded
and that was that. Devastating. Blind panic. I said to a
friend at the time I felt we were speeding towards a brick
wall – but in slow motion. I had no idea how to cope with
the impending collision.

Professor Cunningham recommended palliative
chemotherapy, but before that started we needed to rein-
state the feeding tube.

As Philip describes, it was one of the worst post-
operative weeks. The surgeon who performed the
operation had gone to China and we had a strong sense of
an endgame being played out where different views
clashed. In the end, as difficulties mounted, the hospital
stopped all food.

Constipation became a problem but they could not give
Philip anything for it in case there was an internal leak. He

could not take in any food through the tube as his system
was backed up. A macabre catch-22. I longed for Jervoise
Andreyev to suggest a way forward, but he was on half-
term break. When he returned we had at least established
there was no leak; he prescribed a purge, after which
things reached a kind of equilibrium.

This brought us to the three days of reckoning between
Philip and me. I remember coming in one day to the
Marsden and finding him very low. It was as if the grav-
ity of the situation had defeated him. It was the first time
I had seen him so sad about what was happening and it
devastated me.

There had been many times throughout the previous
four years that Philip had been in pain, brought low by
discomfort, but he had always held out hope – reframed
the situation to eke out a tiny piece of positive news. But
now his illness was closing in on him – on us all – and, for
a moment, he was deeply upset.

Philip had written and spoken a lot about purpose, and
in particular the purpose of his cancer, but at that moment
there seemed to be no purpose – just sadness and loss.

I think all the symptoms he had been suffering took it
out of him. As I watched him suffer I would hate being
powerless against the forces that had taken over his body.
Little is invested in symptom control for cancer sufferers,
and not a lot is written. Most hospitals, including the
Marsden, have excellent palliative care units which deal

expertly with pain control and the symptoms of the dying, but until you are on their horizon it is a hit and miss affair.

Sickness, as a side effect of chemotherapy, is well catered for, but little money goes into Dr Andreyev's area of expertise: the whole gamut of digestive problems arising out of chemotherapy and radiotherapy. It is a miserable list of complaints if ever there was one, and the subject is not often talked about.

Dr Andreyev's work is not curative, but if followed diligently the simple drug routine he offers can transform lives, as it did Philip's. Professor Griffin was very interested in Dr Andreyev's work for his centre, which is why this is one of the two charitable causes that any royalties from this book will help fund.

Philip had always lived his adult life with a plan. It was sometimes invisible to those closest to him but he was normally working on several levels at the same time, playing a long game. This combined with the extraordinary instinct and insight which was his unique gift. His focus groups would be so effective because he not only observed people but got to their motivations, probing until he dragged out the deeper sentiments that characterised their world view beneath the surface flow of opinion.

He would have this effect even on people he met only briefly, as so many letters after his death have testified. In just a short, intense conversation with someone he could arrive at the fundamental truth about them and their purpose and provide an insight or direction that could transform their lives. I keep meeting people – most recently in the departure lounge of Delhi airport at three in the morning – who have stories to tell of Philip's transformative power.

Friends, too, speak of how generous he was with his time – always counselling wisely, getting to the essence of a person and giving them the confidence to achieve what they wanted, and of course giving brilliant advice. In fact, in his last years, while working with Matthew Freud, he mentored a series of politicians, academics and business leaders, moving effortlessly between them until he was too ill to travel. Even then, they would come to him.

Philip's game plan on the matter of his death was not immediately apparent to me or the girls. We knew about his renewed search for purpose but did not know that he was about to go public on death and dying.

I knew he was doing two interviews for the publication of *The Unfinished Revolution*. After being interviewed by Andrew Marr, he called me to say that he thought it had gone well but that there had been a question about his illness at the end; he had got into some 'deep stuff', he said, but did not think it would be broadcast. It was, therefore, a huge shock for us all when we watched the interview on television that Sunday. We were all in tears.

When he gave an interview to Simon Hattenstone of
the *Guardian*, whom I regarded as a master of cutting personal remarks about his subjects, I was uncomfortable. I
thought Philip a bit vulnerable in that department and I
had become more and more protective of him as his health
declined. Yet again Philip was the king of understatement.
The interview had largely been about the book, he said,
'but I got into some heavy stuff about death'.

This interview too turned out to be intensely personal.
Too much so for me, but it was incredibly powerful and is
often referred to in people's letters. It touched a lot of
lives, as did the interview with Andrew Marr. Simon made
a profound connection with Philip and they became
friends, even exchanging texts about football. I remember
one coming in the day before he died.

The next part of the plan revealed itself through Adrian
Steirn, who had teamed up with Matthew Freud on a
project about iconic figures both in South Africa and
worldwide. Adrian was a remarkable photographer and
film-maker and he wanted to photograph Philip and interview him about death. They decided the photograph
would be taken at his grave at Highgate Cemetery.

Part of coming to terms with death for me was preparing for it in the only way I knew how, which was
practically. I told Philip that if he left the funeral to me I
was bound to choose the wrong service or the wrong
music. So it became a joint project entailing many

meetings with Alan Moses and visits to St Margaret's Church. This plan was to include cremation and burial. But first we needed a plot.

The girls wanted somewhere nearby, so they could visit regularly. Philip and I set off for Highgate Cemetery and met the chief gravedigger, Victor Herman, who took us on a tour of his domain. He pointed out various plots but we were clearly not that keen. As we were walking up the hill to the entrance he stopped and said, 'Oh, this one may be free.' It was perfect, right in the middle of things. The sun was shining, the flowers were out and we both felt at peace there.

Back to the office we went, where Victor pulled out a musty old handwritten ledger worthy of Harry Potter, and confirmed that the plot was free. I bought it there and then. Victor has lived his life around death and he combined sensitivity, gravitas and humour in a way that appealed to us and relaxed us both. I genuinely felt we had chosen the right place, a welcoming place.

All this preparation and ritual may seem odd, but for me the practicalities were immensely comforting. It also relaxed Philip, who apart from being insightful was a bit of a control freak. He was reassured that all would be as he wanted it. I knew he worried about me dealing with it alone and didn't want to leave me with any confusion or worry. It also enabled him to envisage his new resting place, which he found peaceful and soothing.

*

Adrian and his team arrived to take Philip to the shoot at 7 a.m. on Thursday 27 October, just eleven days before he was to die. I was worried about the cold and insisted he take a hot-water bottle, a suggestion I think Philip ignored as he was enjoying having so many talented young people around him. I called him continually, knowing how easily he forgot his limits. That Friday we went to the country, where the second part of the interview was to be recorded.

Philip looked very frail and when he walked up the stairs he became a bit breathless. I thought he had caught a chill at the graveyard. By the end of the weekend the breathlessness increased and it was very pronounced on Monday night back at home. I could sense there was something seriously wrong.

The terminal diagnosis loomed in front of us. It was hard not to wonder if this was it. I wanted to call the hospital right away, but Philip insisted on waiting until the morning when we were going in for the chemo that was becoming increasingly difficult for him to tolerate. He was so ill the next morning I called the hospital in advance to arrange an X-ray.

Georgia writes about what happens next. It was the most intense week of my life. All Philip's closest friends came: Tony Blair, Alastair Campbell, Matthew Freud, supportive of us all as ever. His sister, Jill, of course. And friends from all over were in constant touch.

We created our own little world in that intensive care

room, but Philip was fading from us. On his last day of consciousness he asked for his laptop, but he had clips attached to all his fingers and could not type. We took them off and he still could not type, so I said I would type for him. He kept repeating himself and often I would try to tell him he already written something – but he was having none of it. I could hardly bear to listen to his rasping voice, aware of how much every word was taking from him.

He was so intense that day, so fearful, so resisting of death yet also resigned to it. A broken body but a mind still clutching at life – urgent, engaged, desperate to be heard – a life force his cancer-riddled body was trying to extinguish. The previous night he had written on his pad: 'Wonderful the way Grace, Georgia and you held my hand last night. Total blessing.'

Philip knew death was coming, as Georgia writes. His dreams told him. After the dark stuff he said he dreamt of bright shining palaces and multi-coloured works of art, dancing and joyousness, intricate patterns flashing one after another all leading to a road without end. These dreams were, he said, amazing.

I have discussed the moment of Philip's death with many friends, some religious and some most definitely not. It was an incredible moment of bliss as he shuddered and died. It was as if I had glanced at infinity and felt the small hospital room suffused with light. My rational self says I probably imagined all of this – that this moment was a combination of emotional intensity, exhaustion and the Gregorian chant we had listened to for ten hours – but I would like to believe it was Philip's last gift to me as his soul departed.

I am not sure that anyone ever comes to terms with the finality of death. Grief is unpredictable. The first month after Philip died was agony. The grinding, prosaic, formal processes – obtaining the death certificate, probate, making the funeral arrangements – mixing with shock and the inability to grasp what had happened.

For a while after he died, Philip's BlackBerry sat at the side of my bed, flashing red, but only with spam and circulars. It had been his lifeline for so long, his preferred form of communication, that its deadness now seemed only to reflect his loss. Then one night it rang. I was so shocked that I failed to answer it in time. I turned to Philip to say that some idiot who didn't realise he was dead was phoning him in the middle of the night. I had forgotten for a split-second that there was no one to tell.

I can easily see how people might be unable to move on after death. I spent the months after Philip's death feeling truly comfortable only when talking to friends or authors who had been bereaved. I was given reading lists but could concentrate on nothing but poetry. Apart from the medical and feeding paraphernalia, which I got rid of the day after Philip died, I have not been able to move any of his belongings. I fear I am in danger of becoming a little like Miss Havisham. It is the sheer 'gone-ness' that is so impossible to process.

People have asked me why I did not take three months off work after he died. I cannot imagine what they think I would have done with the time. Grieving does not confine itself to specific periods.

I am very busy on Philip's legacy, of which this book is a part, as are the film made by Adrian Steirn and the portrait that can be found on the jacket of this book, which will be part of the National Portrait Gallery's collection. I want to help fund more research and support the charities that are building awareness of oesophageal cancer and how it can be treated and prevented.

I have not worked out the purpose of Philip's death for me, or for our daughters, Georgia and Grace. For us, the core of our life has simply been ripped away.

If we are to make sense of it, then we will do so through Philip's fearlessness in the face of death, his understanding that there is such a thing as a good death, and perhaps somehow, through this book, as he carries on touching people's lives and giving them insights. That was Philip's great gift when he was alive. Let it continue in death.

Letter to a Friend

Alastair Campbell

The High Mass Requiem for Philip Gould was held at All Saints, Margaret Street, London W1 on Tuesday 15 November 2011 before a packed church which included two former prime ministers, who both read lessons, and many other leading political figures. At the request of the family, Alastair Campbell read out the email he had sent his friend just before Philip died. This is the full text of that email.

Dear Philip,
I hope, as do so many others, that somehow you find within you the strength to carry on. The courage you have shown since the day you were told you had cancer

has been inspiring. If anyone can keep on defying the medical odds, you can.

But if this does defeat you this time, I don't want you to go without me saying what a wonderful person you are, and what an extraordinary friend you have been. Of all my friends, you are the one who touches virtually every point of my life – past, present, politics, work, leisure, sport and holidays, education, books, charity, and, more important than anything, family and friendship. I have been blessed to know you. So has Fiona. So have Rory, Calum and Grace. For so many of the happiest moments of our lives, you have been there, indeed often the cause of the happiness.

You've always been there in tough times too. You remember the Alex Ferguson quote: 'The true friend is the one who walks through the door when others are putting on their coats to leave.' You have displayed that brand of friendship so often, so consistently, and with such a force as to keep me going at the lowest of moments.

When I got your moving, lovely message on Tuesday, and was convinced you wouldn't see out the night, I felt like a limb had been wrenched from me. You know my crazy theory that we only know if we have lived a good life as we approach its end – perhaps we only know the real value of a friend when we lose him. The loss for Gail, Georgia and Grace will be enormous. But so many others were touched by you and will share that loss.

My favourite quote of our time in government came not from me or you, or any of the rest of the New Labour team. It came from the Queen in the aftermath of the September 11 attacks ten years ago. 'Grief is the price we pay for love.' You are much loved. There will be much grief. But it is a price worth paying for the joy of having known you, worked with you, laughed with you, cried with you, latterly watched you face death squarely in the eye with the same humility, conviction and concern for others which you have shown in life.

I will always remember you not for your guts in facing cancer, brave though you have been, but for the extraordinary life force you have been in the healthy times. Your enthusiasm, your passion for politics, and belief in its power to do good, your love of Labour, your dedication to the cause and the team – they all have their place in the history that we all wrote together. I loved the defiant tone of your revised *Unfinished Revolution*, your clear message that whatever the critics say, we changed politics and Britain for the better. So often, so many of our people weaken. You never did. You never have. You never would. That is the product of real values, strength of character, and above all integrity of spirit.

In a world divided between givers and takers, you are the ultimate giver. In a world where prima donnas often prosper, you are the ultimate team player. Perhaps alone among the key New Labour people, you have managed to do an amazing job without making enemies. That too is a product of your extraordinary personality, your love of people and your determination always to try to build and heal. It has been humbling to see you, even in these last days and weeks, trying to heal some of the wounds that came with the pressures of power. We can all take lessons from that, and we all should.

Of course I will miss the daily chats, the banter, the unsettled argument about whether QPR are a bigger club than Burnley. More, I'll miss your always being on hand to help me think something through, large or small. But what I will miss more than anything is the life force, the big voice. You have made our lives so much better. You are part of our lives and you will be for ever. Because in my life, Philip, you are a bigger force than the death that is about to take you.

Yours ever,

AC

Acknowledgements

Gail Rebuck

There are many people to thank in the creation of this book. First, Keith Blackmore, who agreed to become the book's editor, taking time off from *The Times* where he is deputy editor and behaving with such compassion and commitment to the project. Ed Victor, friend and agent extraordinaire, for relentlessly championing Philip and his writing and for being such a great neighbour and friend to the whole family. It was while sitting with Ed on our weekly ritual of Sunday afternoon coffee that Philip asked for a 'deadline' for the book, missing the irony of his request.

Alastair Campbell was as close to Philip as it was possible

to be, both as a friend and a political ally, an unfaltering presence, coaxing him on with humour and support. All the Campbells–Millars have been stalwart through these miserable years, an extension of our family, providing respite for us all in France and Scotland. Tony Blair became such a crucial and strong pillar of both spiritual and intellectual support for Philip. He texted us from all over the world and his concern was a great comfort to Philip.

Matthew Freud entered Philip's life in 2000, wearing leather trousers as he recalls, but despite that they became close friends and intellectual sparring partners. Both showed a deep sense of personal integrity and constantly sought out purpose both in their own lives and in those of their clients. All at Freud's have been complete rocks, none more so than Nicola Howson. Matthew and his wife, Liz Murdoch, have become a central pillar in all of our lives and their generosity has no limits. Pete Jones, whom Philip met at university, was a wonderful and constant friend to him all his life.

Thanks through this period also go to Stephen Badger for his spiritual wisdom and support, to David Kamenetzky and Anna-Lena Wetzel, to Noreena Hertz, a founding member of the 'Ask Philip Club', to John Thornton, and to Antonio Lucio who immortalised Philip in a leadership award and continues to be a great friend and mentor. And a very special thank you to all who have contributed to Philip's charities. You know who you are and you will help make Philip's legacy a reality.

Thanks also to Philip's Labour family. The day after he died the house was filled with his political friends: Peter Mandelson, Tessa Jowell, Margaret McDonagh – the New Labour version of the Jewish *shiva*. Our house has been full of letters from party staff, from the politicians Philip spent countless afternoons discussing politics and purpose with: James Purnell, David Miliband, Ed Miliband, Douglas Alexander, Gordon Brown and his friends from No. 10 days, Sally Morgan, Anji Hunter, Peter Hyman and many more he never told me about. I know that the Labour Party was always a home from home for Philip and that the friendships he made there sustained him right through to the end. In his book *The Unfinished Revolution*, Philip thanked so many more who had helped and sustained him.

I would like to thank *The Times* newspaper and James Harding for the beautiful way they presented Philip's words and the support they gave to Philip and this project.

Thanks to the innumerable medical staff who supported Philip through his cancer journey, for the care, kindness and dedication with which they took us through the hardest times. Particular thanks are due to the brilliant Professor Mike Griffin, who operated on Philip when few else could and gave us an extra year, and Claire Sedgwick, who was always at the end of a phone for all the crises. Thanks too to Professor David Cunningham, who never gave up on Philip and lifted us through some of our

darkest days, and all at the Marsden, especially Dr Kaz
Mochlinski, Dr Jervoise Andreyev and Dr Craig Carr, and
all at the Intensive Care Unit.

Thank you too to all those who wrote so beautifully on
Philip's death. Philip had too many close friends to begin
to mention here, but we appreciate deeply all the support
and love we have had over the last few years.

I must also thank my colleagues at Random House for
their support through these difficult times. Thanks to our
authors who have become friends, to Nigella Lawson for
bringing smoked salmon and bagels to feed everyone on
the night Philip died, to Ian McEwan and Annalena
McAfee for insisting I go out when all I wanted to do was
disappear and Carmen Callil who was so supportive
throughout. And thanks to so many more authors for your
words of comfort and inspiration.

A thank you, too, to all at Little, Brown, especially Tim
Whiting for his sensitive editing and to Ursula Mackenzie
for supporting all Philip's projects.

Thank you to my dear friend Susie Figgis, the best
casting director in Britain, for her unwavering support
and for being there on this whole journey, forever at my
side. That is real friendship, built up over forty years. To
my parents and brother, who have known Philip since I
first introduced my gawky university friend nearly forty
years ago and who took him into the family. To Philip's
sister, Jill, who gave him so much comfort in his final
months. And finally to the girls – Georgia and Grace –

the Three Gs, as we are now known – for their love, compassion, humour and wisdom beyond their years. They are Philip's true, lasting legacy.

Keith Blackmore

Editing this book has been a privilege for which I must first and foremost thank Gail Rebuck and Georgia and Grace Gould, whose kindness and patience made it a simple task indeed. Ed Victor's help and advice was, as ever, invaluable. I must also thank my colleagues at *The Times*, especially my indomitable boss and friend, James Harding, for allowing me the time to do it. I am also especially grateful to Roger Alton, Anoushka Healy, Simon Pearson and Anne Spackman for filling whatever gaps I left behind at the paper. Richard Whitehead edited the original newspaper serialisation so thoroughly that my work in that area was greatly reduced. Adrian Steirn kindly gave permission to use material from his interviews. Lastly I must thank my wife, Winifred, and children, Sian and Ben, for putting up with me as I plunged into Philip's extraordinary world for days at a time.

All royalties from this book will go to:
The National Oesophago-Gastric Cancer Fund, to target national awareness of oesophageal cancer and to research early diagnostic tests that could significantly improve life chances.

Donate online at www.justgiving.com/nogcf or by post to:

The National Oesophago-Gastric Cancer Fund
c/o Newcastle Healthcare Charity (Reg. 502473)
Charitable Funds Office
203 Cheviot Court
The Freeman Hospital
High Heaton
Newcastle upon Tyne NE7 7DN

and to:

The Royal Marsden Cancer Charity. This money will support a full-scale study into Dr Andreyev's ground-breaking digestive symptom control protocol for chemotherapy and radiotherapy patients, and Professor Cunningham's cutting-edge research into genetic predisposition to develop oesophageal cancer and appropriate targeted drug responses.

Donate online at www.royalmarsden.org/philipgould or by post to:

The Royal Marsden Cancer Charity
Downs Road
Sutton SM2 5PT

A Short Introduction to Oesophageal/Gastro-oesophageal Cancers

The oesophagus leads from the mouth into the stomach. The tumours that develop in the lower area of the oesophagus, called adenocarcinomas, are commonly grouped with cancers in the area of the gastro-oesophageal junction. Much of the treatment and research work in this field has dealt with these together. They are separate from the different cancers that affect the middle and upper parts of the oesophagus, which require a separate management approach.

In total, every year around half a million people worldwide are diagnosed with oesophageal cancer, and more than four hundred thousand of them die of the disease. It remains very difficult to treat, as frequently it will have spread from the primary tumour site by the time of diagnosis, preventing it from being surgically removed and so requiring any treatment to focus on simply control and containment.

Even when surgery is undertaken with curative intent, the majority of patients suffer recurrences and succumb to their disease. On the most recent data for gastro-oesphageal cancers, five-year survival following surgical resection and peri-operative chemotherapy or post-operative chemo-radiation ranges from 30 to 35 per cent.

And it is a disease that is on the rise. According to Cancer Research UK, there has been a marked increase in the incidence of adenocarcinoma of the lower third of the oesophagus and gastro-oesophageal junction in Britain over the past two to three decades. This is particularly true in Scotland, and most notably among men. The male to female ratio is now more than two to one, making it one of the highest gender differentials of any non-occupational cancer.

The risk of developing the disease also increases with age, with it by far most commonly occurring in the older population. Overall, oesophageal cancer is responsible for almost 3 per cent of all cancers in the United Kingdom and is therefore in the top ten of cancers in this country.

There is undoubtedly scope for improving outcomes, the main factor being earlier diagnosis, before the disease becomes too established in a patient. The problem with this is that the symptoms of early gastro-oesophageal cancer are very common, especially heartburn/indigestion/dyspepsia. It is now being stressed by clinicians that any new symptoms such as these are enough to warrant seeking medical advice. Diagnosis at an early stage should increase the chances of obtaining a cure. But this will also be aided by improving local treatments with enhanced surgical techniques and more modern radiotherapy equipment.

Where the disease recurs or has already spread at the time of diagnosis, there is development work in progress on better general treatments. Combination chemotherapy offers benefits with respect to tumour response and survival when compared to single agent chemotherapy regimens, but this comes at a cost of increased toxicity. The older age of many patients, the fact they are likely to have other common health issues, plus cancer-related debilitation frequently lead to difficulties in successfully applying this approach and it also makes it often problematic to enter these patients into clinical trials.

In order to improve these outcomes and avoid the toxicity of conventional cytotoxic chemotherapy, the focus of many investigators' research has shifted to the use of novel molecular therapies. This involves identifying cell characteristics that will enable targeting treatment very specifically to each individual cancer.

A major example of this is Trastuzumab (herceptin) for patients with gastro-oesophageal cancer that on laboratory analysis is positive for the HER-2 receptor. And the work is going further, beyond cell level, to look at each patient's genetic material. This is heading towards the goal of personalised medicine which will lead to the provision of individually targeted treatments.

This introduction to cancer of the oesophagus was contributed to this book by Dr Kaz Mochlinski and other staff at the Royal Marsden Hospital.

Obituary

The Times

As a full-time political strategist Philip Gould was a pioneer in British politics. In assessing public opinion British party leaders had, before Gould, variously drawn on press proprietors, opinion pollsters, and public relations and advertising men. They had, however, resisted the importation of the American political consultant, and Gould was careful to call himself a strategist not a consultant. He regarded focus groups and market research as an important part of the democratic process, enabling people to speak to their rulers.

He was one of a half dozen crucial figures who helped Neil Kinnock and then Tony Blair and Gordon Brown to modernise the Labour Party. However, his influence was not confined to helping Blair to win the 1997, 2001 and 2005 general elections. He played a continuing role in interpreting public opinion and advising when Blair was Prime Minister. Gould was a force for the professionalisation – some would call it the Americanisation – of the Labour Party.

A workaholic, Gould did not relax easily and found it difficult to read or converse for leisure. He had strong opinions, showed emotions easily and exuded energy. There was something almost bipolar in his shifts between political optimism and pessimism.

His management of focus groups was interventionist, as he interrupted speakers with his questions, directing them to get to the point, usually his point. He was a leader's man, working directly to Blair, who was also impatient with much of the culture and structure of the party.

As a child Gould suffered from dyslexia and he left his secondary modern school in Woking, Surrey, with only one O level. The adolescent Gould was a Labour activist. Both his parents were on the Left politically – his father was a primary school head teacher. As a mature student he studied at evening classes for A levels, eventually gaining a place at Sussex University to study politics and later studying at the LSE. He spent some time in advertising, started an agency which he sold, and then he took a year to study at the London Business School.

Gould's breakthrough came in October 1985 when

Peter Mandelson, Labour's director of campaigns and communications, commissioned him to conduct an audit of the party's communications. The damning report said the party had too many competing and overlapping committees, spent too much of its time speaking to its diminishing number of activists, who were quite unrepresentative of Labour voters, and spurned new communication methods.

Backed by the Labour leader, Neil Kinnock, Gould convened a Shadow Communications Agency (SCA), a group of volunteer media and PR specialists who agreed to supply their services to the party free. Working to Mandelson, Gould's team delivered a professional election campaign that won a great deal of praise in 1987. But it did not stop Labour suffering another bad defeat, its third in succession.

Gould spent much of the 1987 parliament coordinating the SCA and organising polling for the party's policy review. This activity helped to detach Labour from many of its leftist and unpopular policy positions.

He was a firm believer in focus groups, small groups of voters who talked at length about selected topics. Such groups had been regularly used in the commercial world, but rarely in British politics. Gould realised their value and used them as a feedback mechanism, first to Mandelson and later to Blair. The groups revealed the deep fear and distrust of Labour among many ordinary voters and made a profound impression on him.

During the 1992 general election campaign Gould always questioned the reported Labour opinion poll leads; he doubted that the party could be elected given the voters' distrust of it on taxes and its leader. He was furious at John Smith's refusal to abandon Labour's plans to increase spending and taxation and was warned not to annoy Smith any further. The campaign was traumatic for Gould. He worked long hours, visited his dying father almost daily, and the party suffered another defeat.

In the recriminations that followed the election Gould, along with many of the SCA, were made scapegoats for the failings of the politicians and the party organisation. When Smith became party leader Gould was marginalised: party modernisation was no longer fashionable. He was disillusioned.

A formative and uplifting experience was his visit to the US to help Bill Clinton's bid to win the presidency. He learnt important lessons from the US. They included instant rebuttal of opposition attacks and the need for a simple message which the party would reiterate ceaselessly. But he also appreciated that Labour had to change, be seen to change, transcend traditional left-right arguments, and appeal to the new middle-class if it were to survive.

After Smith's death on May 12, 1994, Gould was closely involved in Blair's campaign to win the leadership. Along with Mandelson and Alastair Campbell, he was a key figure in the Blair entourage.

All were tough-minded and devoted to furthering the

'project' of party modernisation. He conducted focus groups and advised Blair, as candidate and then party leader, on how to position himself and what to say.

Gould's task was 'message development'.

He wrote and spoke directly to politicians, linking the polling and focus group material with his own views about political strategy. Blair trusted his reports on the mood of the electorate. He shaped and tested the 1997 election pledges and themes. No other strategist or pollster has had such regular access to a British party leader or Prime Minister.

The subtitle to his book *The Unfinished Revolution* (1998) was 'How the Modernisers Saved the Labour Party', a typically eye-catching claim. Gould drew on his youthful experiences in suburban Woking and how Labour lost touch with the aspiring working-class and emerging middle-class; he called them 'the forgotten people'. His account of how the party 'reconnected' (a favourite word) with them became a bible for young Conservative modernisers who wanted to make their party electable again.

At times his memos made uncomfortable reading for Blair. In 2000 his leaked memo said the public perceived him as 'weak' – 'all spin and no substance' – and the new Labour brand was 'contaminated'. Critics on the Left complained that Gould's concentration on the concerns of wavering Labour voters produced right-wing policy prescriptions and a *Daily Mail* agenda. In the later years of Blair's premiership he regularly warned of voters' worries over crime, immigration and terror. Other critics said his reports were not the voice of the voters but of Gould himself.

Although a steadfast Blairite, Gould advised Blair to announce a date for his departure in 2007 but at a time of his own choosing. He and Campbell, a close friend, persuaded Blair and Brown to mend relations in time for the 2005 general election and later organised talks between the two men to prepare for a smooth handover. The talks collapsed amid mutual recriminations, and Gould was appalled at the attempted coup launched by Brown's supporters in September 2006.

After Brown became prime minister Gould urged him to call an election in autumn 2007, largely on the grounds that the political and economic climate would worsen, and he remained convinced that Labour would have won. He was loyal to Brown in public but thought that he was a poor leader. He was uneasy with some of Brown's associates, finding them conspiratorial.

For at least the first ten years of his association with the party Gould made economic sacrifices, charging the party only his costs. He was independently wealthy because his wife, Gail Rebuck, was chief executive of Random House publishers, and they lived in some style, part of the North London Labour 'glitterati', in a handsome house overlooking Regent's Park.

He conducted research for the private sector and for parties overseas, including the Middle East and Bosnia. In

1998 he joined the board of the *Daily Express*, helping to switch it temporarily to support Labour. In 2004 he was created a life peer and in January 2008 became deputy chairman of Freud Communications, another position of potential influence in the political and media world. But for much of 2008 Gould was recovering from cancer; he was supported by his wide circle of friends, including Blair and Brown, and his wife and daughters. Family was a constant in his life.

He was involved in the 2010 general election campaign, after which the cancer returned. His long and losing battle with cancer was movingly recounted in a series of articles in *The Times*. Shortly before his death he brought out a new edition of *The Unfinished Revolution*, with a foreword by Blair. Both argued for an updated New Labour strategy if the party was to be returned to power.

Gould was an important figure in changing election campaigning in Britain and, indirectly, in other West European states. Like many advisers who are political 'junkies', his rewards came from the excitement and pride at being at the centre of decision-making and having his views respected.

Gould leaves behind his wife, Dame Gail Rebuck, and two daughters.

Philip Gould, political strategist, was born on March 30, 1950. He died of cancer on November 6, 2011, aged 61.

Cast

DR JERVOISE ANDREYEV Consultant gastroenterologist at the Royal Marsden Hospital who has done extensive work dealing with the side effects of cancer treatment.

DR MURRAY F. BRENNAN Leading cancer surgeon at the Memorial Sloan-Kettering Cancer Center in New York City.

DR CRAIG CARR Consultant in intensive care at the Royal Marsden Hospital.

PROFESSOR DAVID CUNNINGHAM World renowned oncologist and head of the gastro–intestinal unit at the Royal Marsden Hospital.

DR ALISTAIR GASCOIGNE Head of intensive care at the Royal Victoria Infirmary, Newcastle.

DR CONOR GILLAN Anaesthetist at the Royal Victoria Infirmary, Newcastle.

PROFESSOR MIKE GRIFFIN Founder of the Northern Oesophago-Gastric Cancer Unit at the Royal Victoria Infirmary, Newcastle, and Professor of Gastrointestinal Surgery at the University of Newcastle upon Tyne.

DR KAZIMIERZ MOCHLINSKI Medical oncologist, specialising in gastro-intestinal cancers at the Royal Marsden Hospital.

MR SATVINDER MUDAN Consultant surgeon and surgical oncologist at the Royal Marsden Hospital.

DR MAURICE SLEVIN Consultant medical oncologist based in London.

DR DAVID STURGEON Consultant to the University College London Psychological Therapies Service, specialising in issues arising from death and dying.

DR DIANA TAIT Consultant clinical oncologist at the Royal Marsden Hospital.